Charles Dickens, Theodore Taylor

Thackeray the Humourist and the Man of Letters

The Story of his Life and literary Labours

Charles Dickens, Theodore Taylor

Thackeray the Humourist and the Man of Letters
The Story of his Life and literary Labours

ISBN/EAN: 9783337108540

Printed in Europe, USA, Canada, Australia, Japan

Cover: Foto ©ninafisch / pixelio.de

More available books at **www.hansebooks.com**

THACKERAY

THE

HUMOURIST AND THE MAN OF LETTERS.

The Story

OF HIS

LIFE AND LITERARY LABOURS,

INCLUDING

A SELECTION FROM HIS CHARACTERISTIC SPEECHES, NOW FOR THE FIRST TIME GATHERED TOGETHER.

By THEODORE TAYLOR, Esq.,

Membre de la Société des Gens de Lettres.

TO WHICH IS ADDED

IN MEMORIAM—By CHARLES DICKENS,

AND

A SKETCH, BY ANTHONY TROLLOPE.

WITH PORTRAIT AND ILLUSTRATIONS.

NEW YORK:
D. APPLETON AND COMPANY,
443 & 445 BROADWAY.
1864.

WILLIAM MAKEPEACE THACKERAY.

A RECENT PHOTOGRAPH BY ERNEST EDWARDS, B.A.

HIS RESIDENCE IN KENSINGTON PALACE GARDENS,

Built after a favourite design in red brick, and similar in style to Old Kensington Palace close by, which was finished in the reign of Queen Anne.

MR. THACKERAY AND THE AGE OF QUEEN ANNE.

(An imaginary sketch made at the Garrick Club many years ago. This portrait of Mr. Thackeray as he used to appear, 12 or 15 years since, is remarkable for its singular excellence, although the hair is represented slightly different from its appearance in later years.)

THE THACKERAY ARMS.

(The professional pen and pencil are made to take the place of a Falcon, the proper family crest; and the favourite spectacles, so generally observed in Mr. Thackeray's early sketches, do service as the motto.)

FAC-SIMILE OF MR. THACKERAY'S HAND-WRITING.

George IV.

He never acted well, by man or woman,
And was as false to his mistress as to his wife.
He deserted his friends and his principles.
He was so ignorant he could scarcely spell;
But he had skill in cutting out coats,
And an undeniable taste for cookery.
He built the palaces of Brighton and of Buckingham,
And for these qualities and proofs of genius,
An admiring aristocracy
Christen'd him the "first gentleman in Europe."
Friends, respect the king whose statue is here,
And the generous aristocracy who admired him.

W M Thackeray

PREFACE.

The following memoir of the late Mr. Thackeray may, perhaps, be acceptable as filling an intermediate place between the newspaper or review article and the more elaborate biography which may be expected in due course. The writer had some peculiar means of acquiring information for the purpose of his sketch, and to this he has added such particulars as have been already made public in English and foreign publications and other scattered sources. The common complaints against memoirs of this necessary haste and incomplete character will not be repeated by those who are accustomed to test questions in morals by the principles which underlie them. That there is nothing necessarily indelicate or improper, in the desire of the public to obtain some personal knowledge of the great and good who have just passed away, is assumed by every daily, weekly, and quarterly journal which on occasions of this kind furnish their readers with such details as they are able to obtain, and which, in no case, confine themselves strictly to the public career of the deceased.

Although some facts in the private life of Mr. Thackeray will be found to be touched upon in these pages, the writer is not conscious of having written a line which could give pain to others.

The writer cannot conclude without acknowledging the kind assistance he has received in furnishing anecdotes and other particulars from Mr. Kinglake, the brilliant historian; Mons. Lacroix; Mr. George Cruikshank, the eminent artist; Mr. Goodlake, Lady Bulwer Lytton, Mr. Moy Thomas, Mr. Blanchard, Mr. George Linley, and others whose names the author is not permitted to mention.

T. T. T.

Grand Hôtel Louvois,
Rue Richelieu, Paris.
25 *Jan.* 1864.

THACKERAY;
THE
HUMOURIST AND THE MAN OF LETTERS.
THE STORY
OF HIS LIFE AND LABOURS.

CHAPTER I.

THACKERAY'S ANCESTORS—DR. THOMAS THACKERAY, HEADMASTER OF HARROW—BISHOP HOADLEY—THEODOSIA WOODWARD—THE ORIGIN OF THE CONNEXION OF THE THACKERAYS WITH INDIA—BIRTH OF THE FUTURE NOVELIST—VOYAGE TO ENGLAND—RECOLLECTION OF NAPOLEON AT ST. HELENA—THE DEATH OF THE PRINCESS CHARLOTTE—HADLEY—THE CHARTERHOUSE—PARTICULARS OF HIS CAREER THERE—CAMBRIDGE—CONDUCTS "THE SNOB," A CAMBRIDGE FACETIOUS MAGAZINE—SPECIMENS OF HIS EARLY CONTRIBUTIONS TO "THE SNOB"—TENNYSON AND JOHN MITCHELL KEMBLE—SOJOURN AT WEIMAR—RECOLLECTIONS OF GOETHE—VISIT TO ROME—DESTINED FOR THE BAR—ART-STUDIES IN PARIS—FRIENDSHIP FOR LOUIS MARVY—THACKERAY'S CRITICISMS ON THE ENGLISH LANDSCAPE PAINTERS.

THE fondness of Mr. Thackeray for lingering amidst the scenes of a boy's daily life in a public grammar school, has generally been attributed to his early education at the Charterhouse, that celebrated monastic-looking establishment in the neighbourhood of Smithfield, which he scarcely disguised from his readers as the original of the familiar "Grey Friars" of his works of fiction. Most of our novelists have given us in various forms their school reminiscences; but none have reproduced them so frequently, or dwelt upon them with such manifest bias towards the subject, as the author of "Vanity Fair," "The Newcomes," and "The Adventures of Philip." It is pleasing to think that this habit, which Mr. Thackeray was well aware had been frequently censured by his critics as carried to excess, was, like his partiality for the times of Queen Anne and the Georges, in some degree due to the traditional reverence of his family for the memory of their great-grandfather, Dr. Thomas Thackeray, the well-remembered headmaster of Harrow. No memoir of William Makepeace Thackeray should begin with any other name than that of this excellent man, who was in every sense the founder of his family. If the evil which men do finds its unhappy consequences in the generations that come after, it is no less true that the life *benè acta*, sows seeds of good of which none can foretell the final fruit. It would not, perhaps, be "considering too curiously," to trace something of the success of his great descendant to that meritorious life of studious industry which secured to the good doctor's family the means of giving to their children, and through them to their children's children, the benefits of culture and good habits.

The memory of Dr. Thomas Thackeray is still held in honour at Harrow among those of the masters who have most contributed to raise the school to the high character it has long enjoyed. The Thackerays came originally from Hampsthwaite, near Knaresborough, in the West Riding of Yorkshire. In this little village Dr. Thomas, the future head-master of Harrow, was born. Of the position in life of the Thackeray family at Hampsthwaite we are not able to give any account; but it is probable that they were of humble means. At all events, Thomas was admitted on the foundation to Eton, from which school he was elected to a scholarship at King's College, Cambridge, in

1711. The Yorkshire lad took degrees and reaped honours rapidly. He was A.B. in 1715, and A.M. in 1719. Subsequently he returned as assistant-master to the school to which he owed his early education, and was a candidate for the provostship of King's College in 1744, when Dr. George was elected. Dr. Thackeray, however, was in most things a fortunate man. In 1746 he succeeded to the head-mastership of Harrow, where he soon made powerful friends. The renown of the school rapidly increased under his rule. He obtained several livings, became Archdeacon of Surrey, and was appointed chaplain to Frederick, Prince of Wales, the dull and despicable father of George III., whom the author of the "Lectures on the Four Georges" sketches with so strong a hand. Dr. Edmund Pyle, of Lynn, in a letter dated 1756, gives some interesting particulars of the Master of Harrow's history. He says: "Dr. Thackeray, who keeps a school at Harrow-on-the-Hill, has one living and fourteen children: a man bred at Eton, and a great scholar in the Eton way, and a good one every way; a true Whig, and proud to be so by some special marks of integrity. He was candidate for the headship of King's, and would have beat all men but George, and George too, if Sir Robert Walpole had not made George's promotion a point. Since this disappointment he took the school at Harrow, to educate his own and other people's children, where he has performed all along with great reputation. The Bishop of Winchester never saw this man in his life, but had heard so much good of him, that he resolved to serve him some way or other if ever he could, but said nothing to anybody. On Friday last, he sent for this Dr. Thackeray, and when he came into the room my Lord gave him a parchment, and told him he had long heard of his good character, and long been afraid he should never be able to give him any serviceable proof of the good opinion he had conceived of him: that what he had put into his hands was the Archdeaconry of Surrey, which he hoped would be acceptable to him, as he might perform the duty of it yearly at the time of his leisure in the Easter holidays. Dr. Thackeray was so surprised and overcome with this extraordinary manner of doing him a favour, that he was very near fainting as he was giving him institution."* This Bishop was the celebrated Hoadley, if we are not mistaken; but Mr. Thackeray could hardly have been aware of this family anecdote when, in his "Lectures on the Four Georges," he somewhat harshly described this unlucky mark for the controversial pamphleteers of his time as "creeping from bishopric to bishopric." Dr. Thackeray's death is announced in the "Gentleman's Magazine" for October, 1760. His widow survived him nearly half a century, and died in January, 1797, in her 90th year. The Doctor had doubtless courted and won her at Eton, in the early days of his studious life. She was Theodosia, the daughter of John Woodward, Esq., of that town and of Butler's Merston, another of whose daughters married Dr. Nicholas Boscawen, Canon of Windsor. Theodosia bore the Doctor six sons and ten daughters, one of whom, the Rev. Elias Thackeray, was Vice-Provost and Bursar of King's College, Cambridge; another son was chaplain at St. Petersburg; another held an appointment in the Customhouse for forty years; and two became Doctors

* Richards's "History of Lynn." 1812.

of Medicine, and settled at Cambridge and Windsor.

The marriages of two of the daughters seem to have laid the foundation of the connexion of the Thackerays with India. Jane married Major Rennell of the East India Company's Service, and Surveyor-General of Bengal; and Henrietta, James Harris, Esq., of the East India Company's Civil Service, and chief of Dacca. The grandfather of the author of "Vanity Fair" was the youngest son of this large family. He was christened, for what reason we do not know, William Makepeace; and it was doubtless by the interest of his sisters' husbands that he also obtained an appointment in the East India Company's Service. William Makepeace married a Miss Webb,* and subsequently retired to England with a competency, leaving behind him his son, Richmond Thackeray, to follow the same career. Richmond obtained a writership in 1797, and suc-

---

* Mr. Hannay tells us that this lady was of the old English family to which the Brigadier Webb of Marlborough's wars belonged, whose portrait is drawn with something of the geniality of kinsmanship in "Esmond."

cessively officiated as Judge and Magistrate of Ranghyr, Secretary to the Board of Revenue at Calcutta, and Collector of the House Tax at Calcutta. Here his son, William Makepeace, the future novelist, was born in 1811—the year before that which gave to the world his illustrious contemporary and fellow-labourer in the field of fiction—Charles Dickens. Mr. Thackeray's father died in Calcutta on the 13th of September, 1815, the very year of the battle of Waterloo, the history of which is so wonderfully interwoven with the story of " Vanity Fair." The son, after remaining in India for some time with his widowed mother, finally bade adieu forever to that country, and was brought to England in 1817. His mother, who had subsequently married Major Carmichael Smyth, still survives, a lady of more than eighty years of age, whose vigorous health and cheerful spirits are proverbial in her son's family.

Sketches of Indian life and Anglo-Indians generally are abundantly interspersed through Mr. Thackeray's writings, but he left India too early to have profited much by Indian experiences. He is said, however, to have retained so strong an impression of the scene of his early childhood, as to have long wished to visit it, and recal such things as were still remembered by him. In his seventh year he was sent to England, when the ship having touched at St. Helena, he was taken up to have a glimpse of Bowood, and there saw that great Captain at whose name the rulers of the earth had so often trembled. It is remarkable that in his little account of the second funeral of Napoleon, which he witnessed in Paris in 1840, no allusion to this fact appears; but he himself has described it in one of his latest works. "When I first saw England," he says, "she was in mourning for the young Princess Charlotte,* the hope of the empire. I came from India as a child, and our ship touched at an island on our way home, where my black servant took me a long walk over rocks and hills, until we reached a garden where we saw a man walking. 'That is he!' cried the black man; 'that is Bonaparte! He eats three sheep every day, and all the children he can lay hands on!' With the

---

* The Princess Charlotte died 6 Nov. 1817.

same childish attendant," he adds, " I remember peeping through the colonnade at Carlton House, and seeing the abode of the Prince Regent. I can yet see the guards pacing before the gates of the palace. The palace! What palace? The palace exists no more than the palace of Nebuchadnezzar. It is but a name now."*

We fancy that Mr. Thackeray was placed under the protection of his grandfather, William Makepeace Thackeray, who had settled with a good fortune, the fruit of his industry in India, at Hadley, near Chipping Barnet, a little village in the churchyard of which lies buried the once-read Mrs. Chapone, the authoress of the " Letters on the Improvement of the Mind," the correspondent of Richardson, and the intimate friend of the learned Mrs. Carter and other blue-stocking ladies of that time.

In the course of time—we believe in his twelfth year—Mr. Thackeray was sent to the Charterhouse School, and remained there as a boarder in the house of Mr. Penny. He appears in the Charterhouse records for the year 1822 as a boy

* " The Four Georges," p. 111.

on the tenth form. In the next year we find him promoted to the seventh form; in 1824 to the fifth; and in 1828, when he had become a day-boy, or one residing with his friends, we find him in the honourable positions of a first-form boy and one of the monitors of the school. He was, however, never chosen as one of the orators, or those who speak the oration on the Founder's Day, nor does he appear among the writers of the Charterhouse odes, which have been collected and printed from time to time in a small volume. The school then enjoyed considerable reputation under the head-mastership of Dr. Russell, whose death happened in the same year as that of his illustrious pupil. No one who has read Mr. Thackeray's novels can fail to know the kind of life he led here. He has continually described his experiences at this celebrated school—the venerable archway into which, in Charterhouse-square, still preserves an interesting token of the old monkish character of the neighbourhood. Only a fortnight before his death he was there again, as was his custom, on the anniversary of the death of Thomas Sutton, the munificent founder of the school. "He was there," says one who has described the scene, "in his usual back seat in the quaint old chapel. He went thence to the oration in the Governor's room; and as he walked up to the orator with his contribution, was received with such hearty applause as only Carthusians can give to one who has immortalized their school. At the banquet afterwards he sat at the side of his old friend and artist-associate in 'Punch,' John Leech; and in a humourous speech proposed, as a toast, the noble foundation which he had adorned by his literary fame, and made popular in his works." "Divine service," says another describer of the scene, for ever memorable as the last appearance of Mr. Thackeray in private life, "took place at four o'clock, in the quaint old chapel; and the appearance of the brethren in their black gowns, of the old stained glass and carving in the chapel, of the tomb of Sutton, could hardly fail to give a peculiar and interesting character to the service. Prayers were said by the Rev. J. J. Halcombe, the reader of the house. There was only the usual parochial chanting of the *Nunc Dimittis;*

the familiar Commemoration-day psalms, 122 and 100, were sung after the third collect and before the sermon; and before the general thanksgiving the old prayer was offered up expressive of thankfulness to God for the bounty of Thomas Sutton, and of hope that all who enjoy it might make a right use of it. The sermon was preached by the Rev. Henry Earle Tweed, late Fellow of Oriel College, Oxford, who prefaced it with the 'Bidding Prayer,' in which he desired the congregation to pray generally for all public schools and colleges, and particularly for the welfare of the house 'founded by Thomas Sutton for the support of age and the education of youth.'"

From Charterhouse School Thackeray went to Trinity College, Cambridge, about 1828, the year of his leaving the Charterhouse, and among his fellow-students there, had Mr. John Mitchell Kemble, the great Anglo-Saxon scholar, and Mr. Tennyson. With the latter—then unknown as a poet—he formed an acquaintance which he maintained to the last, and no reader of the Poet-laureate had a more earnest admiration of his productions than his old Cambridge associate

Mr. Thackeray. At college, Thackeray kept seven or eight terms, but took no degree; though he was studious, and his love of classical literature is apparent in most of his writings, either in his occasional apt two words from Horace, or in the quaint and humorous adoption of Latin idioms in which, in his sportive moods, he sometimes indulged. A recent writer tells us that his knowledge of the classics—of Horace at least—was amply sufficient to procure him an honourable place in the " previous examination."

The earliest of his literary efforts are associated with Cambridge. It was in the year 1829 that he commenced, in conjunction with a friend and fellow-student, to edit a series of humorous papers, published in that city, which bore the title of "The Snob: a Literary and Scientific Journal." The first number appeared on the 9th of April in that year, and the publication was continued weekly. Though affecting to be a periodical, it was not originally intended to publish more than one number; but the project was carried on for eleven weeks, in which period Mr. Lettsom had resigned the entire management to his friend. The contents of each number—which consisted only of four pages of about the size of those of the present volume—were scanty and slight, and consisted entirely of squibs and humorous sketches in verse and prose, many of which, however, show some germs of that spirit of wild fun which afterwards distinguished the "Yellowplush" papers in "Fraser." When completed, the papers bore the following title :—

THE SNOB:

A LITERARY AND SCIENTIFIC JOURNAL.

NOT

"Conducted By Members of the University."

Tityre, tu patulæ recubans sub tegmine fagi
Sylvestrem.   Virgil.

Cambridge:
PUBLISHED BY W. H. SMITH,
ROSE CRESCENT.

1829.

A few specimens of the contents of this curious publication cannot but be interesting to the reader. The first specimen we shall select is a clever skit upon the Cambridge Prize Poem, as follows:

TIMBUCTOO.

TO THE EDITOR OF THE "SNOB."

SIR,—Though your name be "Snob," I trust you will not refuse this tiny "Poem of a Gownsman," which was unluckily not finished on the day appointed for delivery of the several copies of verses on Timbuctoo. I thought, Sir, it would be a pity that such a poem should be lost to the world; and conceiving "The Snob" to be the most widely-circulated periodical in Europe, I have taken the liberty of submitting it for insertion or approbation.

I am, Sir, yours, &c. &c. &c.

TIMBUCTOO.—PART I.

The Situation.

In Africa (a quarter of the world),
Men's skins are black, their hair is crisp and curl'd,

Lines 1 and 2.—See Guthrie's Geography.

The site of Timbuctoo is doubtful; the Author has neatly expressed this in the poem, at the same time giving us some slight hints relative to its situation.

And somewhere there, unknown to public view,
A mighty city lies, called Timbuctoo.

The natural history.

There stalks the tiger,—there the lion roars,   5
Who sometimes eats the luckless blackamoors;
All that he leaves of them the monster throws
To jackals, vultures, dogs, cats, kites, and crows;
His hunger thus the forest monster gluts,
And then lies down 'neath trees called cocoa nuts.   10

The lion hunt.

Quick issue out, with musket, torch, and brand,
The sturdy blackamoors, a dusky band!
The beast is found—pop goes the musketoons—
The lion falls covered with horrid wounds.

Line 5.—So Horace: "*leonum arida nutrix.*"
Line 8.—Thus Apollo:

ελωρια τευχε κυνεσσιν
Οιωνοισι τε πᾶσι.

Lines 5-10.—How skilfully introduced are the animal and vegetable productions of Africa! It is worthy to remark the various garments in which the Poet hath clothed the lion. He is called, 1st, the "Lion;" 2nd, the "Monster" (for he is very large); and 3rd, the "Forest Monarch," which undoubtedly he is.

Lines 11-14.—The author confessed himself under peculiar obligations to Denham's and Clapperton's Travels, as they suggested to him the spirited description contained in these lines.

Line 13.—"Pop goes the musketoons." A learned

Their lives at home.
At home their lives in pleasure always flow, 15
But many have a different lot to know !
Abroad.
They're often caught, and sold as slaves, alas !
Reflections on the foregoing.
Thus men from highest joys to sorrow pass.
Yet though thy monarchs and thy nobles boil
Rack and molasses in Jamaica's isle ; 20
Desolate Afric ! thou art lovely yet ! !
One heart yet beats which ne'er thee shall forget.
What though thy maidens are a blackish brown,
Does virtue dwell in whiter breasts alone ?
Oh no, oh no, oh no, oh no, oh no ! 25
It shall not, must not, cannot, e'er be so.
The day shall come when Albion's self shall feel
Stern Afric's wrath, and writhe 'neath Afric's steel.
I see her tribes the hill of glory mount,
And sell their sugars on their own account. 30
While round her throne the prostrate nations come,
Sue for her rice, and barter for her rum ! 32

friend suggested "Bang" as a stronger expression, but as African gunpowder is notoriously bad, the Author thought "Pop" the better word.

Lines 15–18.—A concise but affecting description is here given of the domestic habits of the people. The infamous manner in which they are entrapped and sold as slaves is described, and the whole ends with an appropriate moral sentiment. The Poem might here finish, but the spirit of the bard penetrates the veil of

This concludes with a like vignette in the "Titmarsh" manner, representing an Indian smoking a pipe of the type once commonly seen in the futurity, and from it cuts off a bright piece for the hitherto unfortunate Africans, as the following beautiful lines amply exemplify.

It may perhaps be remarked that the Author has here "changed his hand." He answers that it was his intention to do so. Before, it was his endeavour to be elegant and concise, it is now his wish to be enthusiastic and magnificent. He trusts the Reader will perceive the aptness with which he has changed his style; when he narrated facts he was calm, when he enters on prophecy he is fervid.

The enthusiasm which he feels is beautifully expressed in lines 25 and 26. He thinks he has very successfully imitated in the last six lines the best manner of Mr. Pope; and in lines 12–26, the pathetic elegance of the author of " Australasia and Athens."

The Author cannot conclude without declaring that his aim in writing this Poem will be fully accomplished, if he can infuse into the breasts of Englishmen a sense of the danger in which they lie. Yes—Africa! If he can awaken one particle of sympathy for thy sorrows, of love for thy land, of admiration for thy virtue, he shall sink into the grave with the proud consciousness that he has raised esteem, where before there was contempt, and has kindled the flame of hope on the mouldering ashes of despair!

shape of a small carved image at the doors of tobacconists' shops. In another paper we find the following pretended

ADVERTISEMENT.

This day is published, price 3s. 6d., "An Essay on the Great Toe," together with the nature and properties of Toes in general, with many sagacious inquiries why the Great Toes are bigger than the Little, and why the Little are less than the Great. Proving also that Gout is not the Dropsy, and that a Gentleman may have a swelled Face without a pain in his Back. Also a Postscript to establish that a Chilblain is very unlike a Lock-jaw. Translated from the original Chaldee.

N.B. A few light summer lectures on Phrenology to be disposed of; enquire of Mr. Smith.

A little further we come upon an exercise in Malapropisms,* under the form of a letter from Mrs.

RAMSBOTTOM IN CAMBRIDGE.

Radish Ground Buildings.—DEAR SIR,—I was surprized to see my name in Mr. Bull's paper, for I give you my word I have not written a syllabub to him since I came to reside here, that I might enjoy the satiety of the literary and learned world.

* Signed "Dorothea Julia Ramsbottom," after Theodore Hook's "Paris Correspondent."

I have the honour of knowing many extinguished persons. I am on terms of the greatest contumacy with the Court of Aldermen, who first recommended your weekly dromedary to my notice, knowing that I myself was a great literati. When I am at home, I make Lavy read it to me, as I consider you the censure of the anniversary, and a great upholder of moral destruction.

When I came here, I began reading Mechanics (written by that gentleman whose name you whistle). I thought it would be something like the "Mechanics' Magazine," which my poor dear Ram used to make me read to him, but I found them very foolish. What do I want to know about weights and measures and bull's eyes, when I have left off trading. I have, therefore, begun a course of ugly physics, which are very odd, and written by the Marquis of Spinningtoes.

I think the Library of Trinity College is one of the most admirable objects here. I saw the busks of several gentlemen whose statutes I had seen at Room, and who all received their edification at that College. There was Aristocracy who wrote farces for the Olympic Theatre, and Democracy who was a laughing philosophy.

I forgot to mention that my son George Frederick is entered at St. John's, because I heard that they take most care of their morals at that College. I called on the tutor, who received myself and son very politely, and said he had no doubt my son would be a tripod, and he hoped perspired higher than polly, which I did not like. I am going to give a tea at my house, when I shall be delighted to see yourself and children.

  Believe me, dear Sir,
   Your most obedient and affectionate,
    DOROTHEA JULIA RAMSBOTTOM.

Further still, we have an example of droll errors in orthography similar to those in which Thackeray afterwards learned to revel in the characters of "Yellowplush," and "Jeames of Buckley Square." This is entitled:—

A STATEMENT OF FAX RELATIVE TO THE LATE MURDER.

By D. J. RAMSBOTTOM.

"Come I to speak in Cæsar's funeral."
Milton. Julius Cæsar, ACT III.

On Wednesday, the 3rd of June, as I was sitting in my back parlour taking tea, young Frederick Tudge entered the room; I reserved from his dislevelled hair and vegetated appearance, that something was praying on his vittels. When I heard from him the cause of his vegetation, I was putrified! I stood transfigured! His father, the editor of "The Snob," had been macerated in the most sanguine manner. The drops of compassion refused my eyes, for I thought of him whom I had lately seen high in health and happiness, that ingenuous indivisable, who often and often when seated alone with me has "made the Table roar," as the poet has it, and whose constant aim in his weakly dromedary, was to delight as well as to reprove. His son Frederick, too young to be acquainted with the art of literal imposition, has commissioned me to excommunicate the circumstances of his death, and call down the anger of the Proctors and Court of Aldermen on the phlogitious perforators of the deed.

It appears he was taking his customary rendezvous by the side of Trumpington Ditch, he was stopped by some men in under-gravy dresses, who put a pitch-plaister on him, which completely developed his nose and eyes, or, as Shakspeare says, "his visible ray." He was then dragged into a field, and the horrid deed was replete! Such are the circumstances of his death; but Mr. Tudge died like Wriggle-us, game to the last; or like Cæsar in that beautiful faction of the poet, with which I have headed my remarks, I mean him who wanted to be Poop of Room, but was killed by two Brutes, and the fascinating hands of a perspiring Senate.

With the most sanguinary hopes that the Anniversary and Town will persecute an inquiry into this dreadful action, I will conclude my repeal to the pathetic reader; and if by such a misrepresentation of fax, I have been enabled to awaken an apathy for the children of the late Mr. Tudge, who are left in the most desultory state, I shall feel the satisfaction of having exorcised my pen in the cause of Malevolence, and soothed the inflictions of indignant Misery.

D. J. RAMSBOTTOM.

P.S. The Publisher requests me to state that the present Number is published from the MS. found in Mr. Tudge's pocket, and one more number will be soon forthcoming, containing his inhuman papers.

About 1831 he repaired to Weimar in Saxony, where, as he describes it, he lived with a score of young English lads, "for study, or sport, or society." Mr. G. H. Lewes, in his "Life of Goethe," tells us that Weimar albums still display with pride the caricatures which the young artist sketched at that period. "My delight in those days" (says Mr. Thackeray), "was to make caricatures for children," a habit, we may add, which he never forgot. Years afterwards, in the fulness of his fame, revisiting the "friendly little Saxon capital," he found, to his great delight, that these were yet remembered, and some even preserved still; but he was much more proud to be told, as a lad, that the great Goethe himself had looked at some of them. In a letter to his friend Mr. Lewes, inserted by the latter in the work referred to, Mr.

Thackeray has given a pleasing picture of this period of his life, and of the society in which he found himself. The Grand Duke and Duchess (he tells us) received the English lads with the kindliest hospitality. The court was splendid, but yet most pleasant and homely. They were invited in turns to dinners, balls, and assemblies there. Such young men as had a right appeared in uniforms, diplomatic and military. Some invented gorgeous clothing: the old Hof Marschall, M. de Spiegel, who (says Mr. Thackeray) had two of the most lovely daughters ever looked on, being in nowise difficult as to the admission of these young Englanders. Of the winter nights they used to charter sedan chairs, in which they were carried through the snow to these court entertainments. Here young Thackeray had the good luck to purchase Schiller's sword, which formed a part of his court costume, and which hung in his study till the day of his death, to put him (as he said) in mind of days of youth the most kindly and delightful.

Here, too, he had the advantage of the society of his friend and fellow-student at Cambridge

Mr. W. G. Lettsom, at present Her Majesty's Chargé d'Affaires at Uruguay, but who was at the period referred to attached to the suite of the English Minister at Weimar. To the kindness of this gentleman he was indebted in a considerable degree for the introductions he obtained to the best families in the town. Mr. Thackeray was always fond of referring to this period of his life. In a private letter written long afterwards, speaking of one of Turner's pictures, he says:—"I recollect, many years ago, at the theatre at Weimar, hearing Beethoven's 'Battle of Vittoria,' in which, amidst a storm of glorious music, the air of 'God save the King' was introduced. The very instant it begun every Englishman in the theatre stood upright, and so stood reverently until the air was finished. Why so? From some such thrill of excitement as makes us glow and rejoice over Mr. Turner and his 'Fighting Téméraire.'"

Devrient, who appeared some years since at the St. James's Theatre in German versions of Shakspeare, was performing at Weimar at that period; and Madame Schröder Devrient was appearing in

Fidelio. In frequenting the performances at the theatres, or attending the levées of the Court ladies, the young students spent their evenings. ".After three and twenty years' absence" (continues Mr. Thackeray) "I passed a couple of summer days in the well-remembered place, and was fortunate enough to find some of the friends of my youth. Madame de Goethe was there, and received me and my daughters with the kindness of old days. We drank tea in the open air at the famous cottage in the park, which still belongs to the family, and had been so often inhabited by her illustrious father. In 1831, though he had retired from the world, Goethe would nevertheless very kindly receive strangers. His daughter-in-law's tea-table was always spread for us. We passed hours after hours there, and night after night with the pleasantest talk and music. We read over endless novels and poems in French, English, and German.   *   *   *
He remained in his private apartment, where only a very few privileged persons were admitted; but he liked to know all that was happening, and interested himself about all strangers.   *   *   *

Of course I remember very well the perturbation of spirit with which, as a lad of nineteen, I received the long-expected intimation that the Herr Geheimrath would see me on such a morning. This notable audience took place in a little ante-chamber of his private apartments, covered all round with antique casts and bas-reliefs. He was habited in a long grey or drab redingote, with a white neckcloth and a red riband in his buttonhole. He kept his hands behind his back, just as in Rauch's statuette. His complexion was very bright, clear, and rosy; his eyes extraordinarily dark, piercing, and brilliant. I felt quite afraid before them, and recollect comparing them to the eyes of the hero of a certain romance called 'Melmoth the Wanderer,' which used to alarm us boys thirty years ago; eyes of an individual who had made a bargain with a certain person, and at an extreme old age retained these eyes in all their awful splendour. I fancied Goethe must have been still more handsome as an old man than even in the days of his youth. His voice was very rich and sweet. He asked me questions about myself, which I answered as best I could.

I recollect I was at first astonished, and then somewhat relieved, when I found he spoke French with not a good accent. *Vidi tantum.* I saw him but three times. Once walking in the garden of his house in the Frauenplan; once going to step into his chariot on a sunshiny day, wearing a cap, and a cloak with a red collar. He was caressing at the time a beautiful little golden-haired granddaughter, over whose sweet fair face the earth has long since closed too. Many of us who had books or magazines from England sent them to him, and he examined them eagerly. 'Fraser's Magazine' had lately come out, and I remember he was interested in those admirable outline portraits which appeared for a while in its pages. But there was one, a very ghastly caricature of Mr. R——,* which, as Madame de Goethe told me, he shut up and put away from him angrily. 'They would make me look like that,' he said; though in truth I can fancy nothing more serene, majestic, and *healthy*-looking than the grand old Goethe. Though his sun was setting, the sky round about was calm and bright,

---

* Samuel Rogers, the poet.

and that little Weimar illumined by it. In every one of those kind *salons* the talk was still of art and letters. * * * *
At court the conversation was exceedingly friendly, simple, and polished. The Grand Duchess (the present Grand Duchess Dowager), a lady of very remarkable endowments, would kindly borrow our books from us, lend us her own, and graciously talk to us young men about our literary tastes and pursuits. In the respect paid by this court to the patriarch of letters there was something ennobling, I think, alike to the subject and sovereign. With a five-and-twenty years' experience since those happy days of which I write (says Mr. Thackeray) and an acquaintance with an immense variety of human kind, I think I have never seen a society more simple, charitable, courteous, gentlemanlike, than that of the dear little Saxon city where the good Schiller and the great Goethe lived and lie buried." *

The Weimar reminiscences show how early

---

* The whole of this long and beautiful letter may be read in Mr. Lewes's biography of "the Great Goethe," a cheap edition of which has just been published.

his passion for art had developed itself. One who knew him well affirms that he was originally intended for the bar; but he had, indeed, already determined to be an artist, and for a considerable period he diligently followed his bent. He visited Rome, where he stayed some time, and subsequently, as we shall see, settled for a considerable time in Paris, where, says a writer in the "Edinburgh Review" for January, 1848, "we well remember, ten or twelve years ago, finding him, day after day, engaged in copying pictures in the Louvre, in order to qualify himself for his intended profession. It may be doubted, however," adds this writer, "whether any degree of assiduity would have enabled him to excel in the money-making branches, for his talent was altogether of the Hogarth kind, and was principally remarkable in the pen-and-ink sketches of character and situation which he dashed off for the amusement of his friends." This is just criticism; but Thackeray, though caring little himself for the graces of good drawing or correct anatomy, had a keen appreciation of the beauties of his contemporary artists. Years after—in 1848—when, as he says, the revolutionary storm which raged in France "drove many peaceful artists, as well as kings, ministers, tribunes, and socialists of state for refuge to our country," an artist friend of his early Paris life found his way to Thackeray's home in London. This was Monsieur Louis Marvy, in whose *atelier* the former had passed many happy hours with the family of the French artist—in that constant cheerfulness and sunshine, as his English friend expressed it, which the Parisian was now obliged to exchange for a dingy parlour and the fog and solitude of London. A fine and skilful landscape painter himself, M. Marvy, while here, as a means of earning a living, made a series of engravings after the works of our English landscape painters. For some of these his friend obtained for M. Marvy permission to take copies in the valuable private collection of Mr. Thomas Baring. The publishers, however, would not undertake the work without a series of letter-press notices of each picture from Mr. Thackeray; and the latter accordingly added some criticisms which are interesting as developing his theory of this kind of art. The artists whose works are engraved are Calcott, Turner, Holland, Danby, Creswick, Collins, Redgrave, Lee, Cattermole, W. J. Müller, Harding, Nasmyth, Wilson, E. W. Cooke, Constable, De Wint, and Gainsborough. Of Turner he says:—" Many cannot comprehend the pictures themselves, but stand bewildered before those blazing wonders, those blood-red shadows, those whirling gamboge suns—awful hieroglyphics, which even the Oxford undergraduate (Mr. Ruskin), Turner's most faithful priest and worshipper, cannot altogether make clear. Nay, who knows whether the prophet himself has any distinct idea of the words which break out from him as he sits whirling on the tripod, or of what spirits will come up as he waves his wand and delivers his astounding incantation? It is not given to all to understand; but at times we have glimpses of comprehension, and in looking at such pictures as the 'Fighting Téméraire' for instance, or the 'Star Ship,' we admire, and can scarce find words adequate to express our wonder at the stupendous skill and genius of this astonishing master. If those words which we think we understand are sublime, what are those others which are unintelligible? Are they sublime too, or have they reached that next and higher step which by some is denominated ridiculous! Perhaps we have not arrived at the right period for judging, and Time, which is proverbial for settling quarrels, is also required for sobering pictures." Of Danby he says, "His pictures are always still. You stand before them alone, and with a hushed admiration, as before a great landscape when it breaks on your view." On Constable's well-known picture of the Cornfield in the National Gallery he says: "The beautiful piece of autumn appears to be under the influence of a late shower. The shrubs, trees, and distance are saturated with it. What a lover of water that youngster must be who is filling himself within after he has been wetted to the skin by the rain which has just passed away. As one looks at this delightful picture one cannot but admire the manner in which the specific character of every object is made out: the undulations of the ripe corn, the chequered light on the road, the freshness of the banks, the trees and their leafage, the brilliant cloud, awfully contrasting against the trees, and here and there broken with azure." Such were the opinions of the author of the grotesque illustrations of "Vanity Fair" and "Pendennis" upon those great landscape painters of whom England is proud—opinions which show at least a warm sympathy with that higher order of art in which he had failed to achieve a satisfactory degree of success.

Facsimile of the little vignette in the Cambridge "Snob."
See above, page 19.

CHAPTER II.

EARLY CONNEXION WITH FRASER'S MAGAZINE—RESIDENCE IN ALBION-STREET—FONDNESS FOR PARIS LIFE—ANECDOTE OF A VISIT TO THAT CITY WHEN A BOY—THE QUARTIER LATIN—KINDNESS TO OLD ACQUAINTANCES IN PARIS — ANECDOTES OF SUBSEQUENT VISITS TO FRANCE — DISLIKE OF FRENCH INSTITUTIONS — THE PARADISE OF YOUNG PAINTERS—HIS ACCOUNT OF ART-STUDENT LIFE IN PARIS—OPINIONS ON THE FRENCH SCHOOL OF PAINTING—GROWING LOVE OF AUTHORSHIP—PICKWICK—MACAULAY—EARLY OPINIONS ON THE OLD NOVELISTS—PREFERENCE FOR NOVELS OVER HISTORY—MAGINN AND "FRASER'S MAGAZINE"—MACLISE'S PICTURE OF THE FRASERIANS IN 1834—FATHER PROUT—ORIGIN OF THE YELLOWPLUSH IDEA.

IT was, we believe, in 1834, and while residing for a short period in Albion-street, Hyde Park, the residence of his mother and her second husband, Major Carmichael Smyth, that Mr.

Thackeray began his literary career as a contributor to "Fraser's Magazine." The pseudonims of "Michael Angelo Titmarsh," "Fitz Boodle," "Yellowplush," or "Lancelot Wagstaff," under which he afterwards amused the readers of the periodicals, had not then been thought of. His early papers were chiefly relating to the Fine Arts; but most of them had some reference to his French experiences. He seems to have had a peculiar fancy for Paris, where he resided, with brief intervals, for some years after coming of age, and where most of his magazine papers were written. In one of those delightful essays in which he makes his reader the confidants of his personal reminiscences, he has given us an amusing anecdote of his first furtive trip to that capital. He tells us how, when a lad of nineteen, he found himself one day at a certain inn in Dover, whose exorbitant charges he more than once in his writings touches on for the benefit of his readers, and how, having paid his coach-fare to London, the bill of that unreasonable hostelry reduced his allowance so low, that a bare half-crown for the customary fee to coachman was all that remained. It was in the Easter vacation of his Cambridge life, and he had just returned from Paris, where he had been without leave of his friends : an awful sense of guilt weighed on his mind. The possession of a spare twenty pounds, and the wish to see a friend in Paris, had proved temptations too strong to be resisted. But the worst part of the case was the fact that he had prevaricated with his College tutor—told him, in fact, a fib; for, having been asked by him where he intended to spend his holidays, he had answered with a friend in Lincolnshire. Telling this anecdote more than thirty years afterwards, he humorously adds : " Guilt, sir —guilt always remained stamped on the memory; and I feel easier in my mind now that it is liberated of this old peccadillo."

A recent writer has given some amusing particulars of his Paris life, and his subsequent interest in the city, where he had many friends and was known to a wide circle of readers. " He lived," says the writer, " in Paris ' over the water,' and it is not long since, in strolling about the Latin Quarter with the best of companions, that we visited his lodgings, Thackeray inquiring after those who were already forgotten—unknown. Those who may wish to learn his early Parisian life and associations should turn to the story of 'Philip on his Way through the World.' Many incidents in that narrative are reminiscences of his own youthful literary struggles whilst living modestly in this city. Latterly, fortune and fame enabled the author of 'Vanity Fair' to visit imperial Paris in imperial style, and Mr. Thackeray put up generally at the Hôtel de Bristol in the Place Vendôme. Never was increase of fortune more gracefully worn or more generously employed. The struggling artist and small man of letters whom he was sure to find at home or abroad, was pretty safe to be assisted if he learned their wants. I know of many a kind act. One morning, on entering Mr. Thackeray's bedroom in Paris, I found him placing some napoleons in a pill-box, on the lid of which was written, 'One to be taken occasionally.' 'What are you doing?' said I. 'Well,' he replied, 'there is an old person here who says she is very ill and in distress, and I strongly suspect that this is the sort of medicine she wants. Dr. Thackeray intends to leave it with her himself. Let us walk out together.' * Thackeray used to say that he came to Paris for a holiday and to revive his recollections of French cooking. But he generally worked here, especially when editing the 'Cornhill Magazine.'" †

Thackeray's affection for Paris, however, appears to have been founded upon no relish for the gaieties of the French metropolis, and certainly not upon any liking for French institutions. His papers on this subject are generally criticisms upon political, social, and literary failings of the French, written in a severe spirit which savours more of the confident judgment of youth than of the calm spirit of the citizen of the world. The reactionary rule of Louis Philippe, the Government of July, and the boasted charter of 1830, were the objects of his especial dislike; nor was he less unsparing in his views of French morals as exemplified in their law courts, and in the novels of such writers as Madame Dudevant. The truth is, that at this period Paris was, in the

* A similar story has been told of Goldsmith, which, however, may have suggested the pill-box remedy in the instance in the text.

† Paris Correspondent, *Morning Post*.

eyes of the art student, simply the Paradise of young painters. Possessed of a good fortune—said to have amounted on his coming of age in 1832 to £20,000—the young Englishman passed his days in the Louvre, his evenings with his French artist acquaintances, of whom his preface to Louis Marvy's sketches gives so pleasant a glimpse; or sometimes in his quiet lodgings in the Quartier Latin, in dashing off for some English or foreign paper his enthusiastic notices of the Paris Exhibition, or a criticism on French writers, or a story of French artist life, or an account of some great *cause célèbre* then stirring the Parisian world. This was doubtless the happiest period of his life. In one of these papers he describes minutely the life of the art student in Paris, and records his impressions of it at the time.

"To account (he says) for the superiority over England—which, I think, as regards art, is incontestable—it must be remembered that the painter's trade, in France, is a very good one; better appreciated, better understood, and, generally, far better paid than with us. There are a dozen excellent schools in which a lad may enter here, and, under the eye of a practised master, learn the apprenticeship of his art at an expense of about ten pounds a-year. In England there is no school except the 'Academy,' unless the student can afford to pay a very large sum, and place himself under the tuition of some particular artist. Here a young man for his ten pounds has all sorts of accessory instruction, models, &c.; and has further, and for nothing, numberless incitements to study his profession which are not to be found in England; the streets are filled with picture-shops, the people themselves are pictures walking about; the churches, theatres, eating-houses, concert-rooms, are covered with pictures; Nature itself is inclined more kindly to him, for the sky is a thousand times more bright and beautiful, and the sun shines for the greater part of the year. Add to this, incitements more selfish, but quite as powerful: a French artist is paid very handsomely; for five hundred a-year is much where all are poor; and has a rank in society rather above his merits than below them, being caressed by hosts and hostesses in places where titles are laughed at, and a baron is thought of no more account than a banker's clerk.

"The life of the young artist here is the easiest, merriest, dirtiest existence possible. He comes to Paris, probably at sixteen, from his province; his parents settle forty pounds a-year on him, and pay his master; he establishes himself in the Pays Latin, or in the new quarter Nôtre Dame de Lorette (which is quite peopled with painters); he arrives at his *atelier* at a tolerably early hour, and labours among a score of companions as merry and poor as himself. Each gentleman has his favourite tobacco-pipe, and the pictures are painted in the midst of a cloud of smoke, and a din of puns and choice French slang, and a roar of choruses, of which no one can form an idea who has not been present at such an assembly." In another paper he discourses enthusiastically of the French school of painting as exemplified in a picture in the Exhibition by Carel Dujardin, as follows:—

"A horseman is riding up a hill, and giving money to a blowsy beggar-wench. *O matutini rores auræque salubres!* in what a wonderful way has the artist managed to create you out of a few bladders of paint and pots of varnish. You can see the matutinal dews twinkling in the grass, and feel the fresh, salubrious airs ('the breath of Nature blowing free,' as the Corn-law-man sings) blowing free over the heath. Silvery vapours are rising up from the blue lowlands. You can tell the hour of the morning and the time of the year; you can do anything but describe it in words. As with regard to the Poussin above-mentioned, one can never pass it without bearing away a certain pleasing, dreaming feeling of awe and musing; the other landscape inspires the spectator infallibly with the most delightful briskness and cheerfulness of spirit. Herein lies the vast privilege of the landscape painter; he does not address you with one fixed particular subject or expression, but with a thousand never contemplated by himself, and which only arise out of occasion. You may always be looking at a natural landscape as at a fine pictorial imitation of one; it seems eternally producing new thoughts in your bosom, as it does fresh beauties from its own."

It is certain that he had developed a talent for writing long before he had abandoned his intention of becoming a painter, and that he became a contributor to magazines at a time when there was at least no necessity for his earning a livelihood by his pen. It is probable, therefore, that it was his success in the literary art, rather than his failure, as has been assumed, in acquiring skill as a painter, which gradually drew him into that career of authorship, the pecuniary profits of which became afterwards more important to him. Other papers of his, written at this undecided period of his life, contain numerous interesting evidences of his growing love of literature. Of his contemporary English writers he has much to say. "Pickwick," and "Nicholas Nickleby," then publishing, are frequently mentioned. We have seen how he quotes the Corn Law Rhymer, then but little known to the English public. Speaking of the French he says, "They made Tom

Paine a deputy; and as for Tom Macaulay they would make a dynasty of him." In a paper " On French fashionable Novels," in an American newspaper, of which he was the Paris correspondent, he thus alludes to the circulating libraries of Paris, from which he obtained his supply of contemporary reading :—

"Twopence a volume bears us whithersoever we will ;—back to Ivanhoe and Cœur de Lion, or to Waverley and the Young Pretender, along with Walter Scott; up to the heights of fashion with the charming enchanters of the silver-fork school; or, better still, to the snug inn parlour or the jovial tap-room, with Mr. Pickwick and his faithful Sancho Weller.

"I am sure that a man who, a hundred years hence, should sit down to write the history of our time, would do wrong to put that great contemporary history of 'Pickwick' aside, as a frivolous work. It contains true character under false names; and, like 'Roderick Random,' an inferior work, and 'Tom Jones' (one that is immeasurably superior), gives us a better idea of the state and ways of the people, than one could gather from any more pompous or authentic histories."

In another paper on Caricatures and Lithography, in the same journal, containing a kindly allusion to his friend, George Cruikshank, he developes this idea further, giving us a still more interesting view of his reading, and of his growing preference for fiction over other forms of literature. "At the close," he says, " of his history of George II., Smollet condescends to give a short chapter on Literature and Manners. He speaks of Glover's 'Leonidas,' Cibber's 'Careless Husband,' the poems of Mason, Gray, the two Whiteheads, 'the nervous style, extensive erudition, and superior sense of a Cooke; the delicate taste, the polished muse, and tender feeling of a Lyttelton.' 'King,' he says, 'shone unrivalled in Roman eloquence, the female sex distinguished themselves by their taste and ingenuity. Miss Carter rivalled the celebrated Dacier in learning and critical knowledge; Mrs. Lennox signalized herself by many successful efforts of genius, both in poetry and prose; and Miss Reid excelled the celebrated Rosalba in portrait painting, both in miniature and at large, in oil as well as in crayons. The genius of Cervantes was transferred into the novels of Fielding, who painted the characters and ridiculed the follies of life with equal strength, humour and propriety. The field of history and biography was cultivated by many writers of ability, among whom we distinguish the copious Guthrie, the circumstantial Ralph, the laborious Carte, the learned and elegant Robertson, and above all, the ingenious, penetrating, and comprehensive Hume,' &c. &c. We will quote no more of the passage. Could a man in the best humour sit down to write a graver satire? Who cares for the tender muse of Lyttelton? Who knows the signal efforts of Mrs. Lennox's genius? who has seen the admirable performances, in miniature and at large, in oil as well as in crayons, of a Miss Reid? Laborious Carte, and circumstantial Ralph, and copious Guthrie, where are they, their works, and their reputation? Mrs. Lennox's name is just as clean wiped out of the list of worthies as if she had never been born; and Miss Reid, though she was once actual flesh and blood, 'rival in miniature and at large' of been at all; her little farthing rushlight of a soul and reputation having burnt out, and left neither wick nor tallow. Death, too, has overtaken copious Guthrie and circumstantial Ralph. Only a few know whereabouts is the grave where lies laborious Carte; and yet, oh! wondrous power of genius! Fielding's men and women are alive, though history's are not. The progenitors of circumstantial Ralph, sent forth, after much labour and pains of mating, educating, feeding, clothing, a real man-child—a great palpable mass of flesh, bones, and blood (we say nothing about the spirit), which was to move through the world, ponderous, writing histories, and to die, having achieved the title of circumstantial Ralph; and lo! without any of the trouble that the parents of Ralph had undergone, alone, perhaps, in a watch or spunging-house, fuddled, most likely, in the blandest, easiest, and most good-humoured way in the world, Henry Fielding makes a number of men and women on so many sheets of paper, not only more amusing than Ralph or Miss Reid, but more like flesh and blood, and more alive now than they.

"Is not Amelia preparing her husband's little supper? Is not Miss Snap chastely preventing the crime of Mr. Firebrand? Is not Parson Adams in the midst of his family, and Mr. Wild taking his last bowl of punch with the Newgate Ordinary? Is not every one of them a real substantial *have*-been personage now?— more real than Reid or Ralph? For our parts, we will not take upon ourselves to say that they do not exist somewhere else; that the actions attributed to them have not really taken place; certain we are that they are more worthy of credence than Ralph, who may or may not have been circumstantial;—who may or may not even have existed, a point unworthy of disputation. As for Miss Reid, we will take an affidavit that neither in miniature nor at large did she excel the celebrated Rosalba; and with regard to Mrs. Lennox, we consider her to be a mere figment, like Narcissa, Miss Tabitha Bramble, or any hero or heroine depicted by the historian of "Peregrine Pickle.'"

Mr. Thackeray had scarcely attained the age

of three-and-twenty when the young literary art-student in Paris was recognised as an established contributor of "Fraser," worthy to take a permanent place among that brilliant staff which then rendered this spirited periodical famous both in England and on the continent. It was then under the editorship of the celebrated Maginn, one of the last of those compounds of genius and profound scholarship, with reckless extravagance and loose morals, who once flourished under the encouragement of a tolerant public opinion. There can be no doubt that the editor and Greek scholar, who is always in difficulties, who figures in several of his works, is a faithful picture of this remarkable man as he appeared to his young contributor. His friend, Mr. Hannay, says:—

"Certain it is, that he lent—or in plainer English—gave—five hundred pounds to poor old Maginn, when he was beaten in the battle of life, and like other beaten soldiers made a prisoner—in the fleet. With the generation going out,—that of Lamb and Coleridge,—he had, we believe, no personal acquaintance. Sydney Smith he met at a later time; and he remembered with satisfaction that something which he wrote about Hood gave pleasure to that delicate humourist and poet in his last days. But his first friends were the Fraserians, of whom Father Prout,— always his intimate,—and Carlyle,—always one of his most appreciating friends,—survive. From reminiscences of the wilder lights in the 'Fraser' constellation were drawn the pictures of the queer fellows connected with literature in 'Pendennis,' —Captain Shandon, the ferocious Bludyer, stout old Tom Serjeant, and so forth. Magazines in those days were more brilliant than they are now, when they are haunted by the fear of shocking the Fogy element in their circulation; and the effect of their greater freedom is seen in the buoyant, riant, and unrestrained comedy of Thackeray's own earlier 'Fraser' articles. 'I suppose we all begin by being too savage,' is the phrase of a letter he wrote in 1849; '*I know one who did.*' He was alluding here to the 'Yellowish Papers' in particular, where living men were very freely handled. This old, wild satiric spirit it was which made him interrupt even the early chapters of 'Vanity Fair,' by introducing a parody, which he could not resist, of some contemporary novelists." *

But we have a proof of the fact of how fully he was recognised by his brother Fraserians as of themselves in Maclise's picture of the Fraser contributors, prefixed to the number of " Fraser's Magazine," for January, 1835—a picture which must have been drawn at some period in the previous year. This picture represents a banquet at the house of the publisher, Mr. Fraser, at which, on some of his brief visits to London, Thackeray had doubtless been present, for it is easy to trace in the juvenile features of the tall figure with the double eyeglass—Mr. Thackeray was throughout life somewhat near-sighted—a portrait of the future author of " Vanity Fair." Mr. Mahony, the well-known " Father Prout " of the magazine, in his account of the picture written in 1859, tells us that the banquet was

* *Edinburgh Evening Courant*, Jan. 5, 1864.

no fiction. In the chair appeared Dr. Maginn in the act of making a speech; and around him, among a host of contributors, including Bryan Walker Procter, (better known then as Barry Cornwall), Robert Southey, William Harrison Ainsworth, Samuel Taylor Coleridge, James Hogg, John Galt, Fraser the publisher, having on right, Mr. Lockart, Theodore Hook, Sir David Brewster, Thomas Carlyle, Sir Egerton Brydges, Rev. — Gleig, Edward Irving, and others, numbering twenty-seven in all—of whom, in 1859, eight only were living.

This celebrated cartoon of the Fraserians appears to place Mr. Thackeray's connexion with the Magazine before 1835; but we have not succeeded in tracing any contribution from his hand earlier than Nov. 1837. Certainly, the afterwards well-used *noms de plume* of Michael Angelo Titmarsh, Fitzboodle, Charles Yellowplush, and Ikey Solomons, are wanting in the earlier volumes.

It is in the number for the month and year referred to that we first find him contributing a paper which is not reprinted in his "Miscellanies," and which is interesting as explaining the origin of that assumed character of a footman in which the author of the "Yellowplush Papers" and "Jeames's Diary" afterwards took delight. A little volume had been published in 1837, entitled "My Book; or the Anatomy of Conduct by John Henry Skelton." The writer of this absurd book had been a woollen draper in the neighbourhood of Regent-street. He had become possessed of the fixed idea that he was destined to become the instructor of mankind in the true art of etiquette. He gave parties to the best company whom he could induce to eat his dinners and assemble at his conversaziones, where his amiable delusion was the frequent subject of the jokes of his friends. Skelton, however, felt them little. He spent what fortune he had, and brought himself to a position in which his fashionable acquaintances no longer troubled him with their attentions; but he did not cease to be, in his own estimation, a model of deportment. He husbanded his small resources, limiting himself to an humble dinner daily, at a coffee-house in the neighbourhood of his old home, where his perfectly fitting dress-coat—for in this article he was still enabled to shine—his brown wig and dyed whiskers, his ample white cravat of the style of the Prince Regent's days, and his well polished boots, were long destined to raise the character of the house on which he bestowed his patronage. In the days of his prosperity, Skelton was understood among his acquaintances to be engaged on a work which should hand down to posterity the true code of etiquette—that body of unwritten law which regulated the society of the time of his favourite monarch. In the enforced retirement of his less prosperous days, the woollen-draper's literary design had time to develop itself, and in the year 1837, "My Book; or the Anatomy of Conduct by John Henry Skelton," was finally given to the world.

It was this little volume which fell in the way of Thackeray, who undertook to review it for "Fraser's Magazine." In order to do full justice to the work, nothing seemed more proper than to present the reviewer in the assumed character of a fashionable footman. The review, therefore, took the form of a letter from Charles Yellowplush, Esq., containing "Fashionable fax and polite Annygoats," dated from "No. ——, Grosvenor Square, (N.B.—Hairy Bell)," and addressed to Oliver Yorke, the well-known pseudonym of the Editor of "Fraser." To this accident may be attributed those extraordinary efforts of cicography which had their germ in the Oxford "Snob," but which attained their full development in the Miscellanies, the Ballads, the Snob papers, and other short works, and also in some portions even of the latest of the author's novels. The precepts and opinions of "Skelton," or "Skeleton," as the reviewer insisted on calling the author of the "Anatomy," were fully developed and illustrated by Mr. Yellowplush. The footman who reviewed the "fashionable world," achieved a decided success. Charles Yellowplush was requested by the editor to extend his comments upon society and books, and in January, 1838, the "Yellowplush Papers " were commenced, with those peculiar rude illustrations by the author, which appear at first to have been suggested by the style of Maclise's portraits in the same magazine, but which afterwards became habitual to him.

CHAPTER III.

ILLUSTRATIONS OF THE PICKWICK PAPERS—ROYAL ACADEMY EXHIBITION—DICKENS—EXECUTIONS IN PARIS—RETURN TO LONDON—PARIS LETTERS—MARRIAGE—YELLOWPLUSH PAPERS—OTHER WRITINGS—CONTRIBUTIONS TO THE WESTMINSTER—PARIS SKETCH BOOK—SECOND EDITION—HISTORY OF SAMUEL TITMARSH—FITZ-BOODLE'S CONFESSIONS—CONTRIBUTIONS TO MAGAZINES—NOTES OF A JOURNEY FROM CORNHILL TO CAIRO—WRITINGS FOR PUNCH—OTHER WORKS.

It was in the year 1836 that Mr. Thackeray, according to an anecdote related by himself, offered Mr. Dickens to undertake the task of illustrating one of his works. The story was told by the former at an anniversary dinner of the Royal Academy a few years since, Mr. Dickens being present on the occasion. "I can remember (said Mr. Thackeray) when Mr. Dickens was a very young man, and had commenced delighting the world with some charming humorous works in covers, which were coloured light green, and came out once a month, that this young man wanted an artist to illustrate his writings; and I recollect walking up to his chambers in Furnival's Inn, with two or three drawings in my hand, which, strange to say, he did not find suitable. But for the unfortunate blight which came over my artistical existence, it would have been my pride and my pleasure to have endeavoured one day to find a place on these walls for one of my performances." The work referred to was the "Pickwick Papers," which were originally commenced in April of that year, as the result of an agreement with Mr. Dickens and Mr. Seymour, the comic artist—the one to write, and the other to illustrate, a book which should exhibit the adventures of cockney sportsmen. As our readers know, the descriptive letterpress, by the author of the "Sketches by Boz," soon attracted the attention of the world; while the clever illustrations by Seymour, which had the merit of creating the well-known pictorial characteristics of Mr. Pickwick and his friends, became regarded only as illustrations of the new humourist's immortal work. Unhappily, only two or three monthly numbers had been completed, when Seymour destroyed himself in a fit of derangement. A new artist was wanted, and the result was the singular interview between the two men whose names, though representing schools of fiction so widely different, were destined to become constantly associated in the public mind. Mr. Dickens was then entering into that great fame as a writer of fiction which has never flagged from that time. The young artist had scarcely attempted literature, and had still before him many years of obscurity. The slow growth of his fame presents a curious contrast to the career of his fellow-novelist. So much as Mr. Thackeray subsequently worked in contributing to " Fraser," in co-operating with others on daily newspapers, in writing for " Cruikshank's Comic Almanac," for the " Times " and the " Examiner," for " Punch," and for the " Westminster " and other Reviews, it could not be said that he was really known to the public till the publication of " Vanity Fair," when he had been an active literary man for at least ten years, and had attained the age of thirty-seven. The "Yellowplush Papers," in "Fraser," enjoyed a sort of popularity, and were at least widely quoted in the newspapers; but of their author few inquired. Neither did the two volumes of the "Paris Sketch Book," though presenting many good specimens of his peculiar humour, nor the account of the second funeral of Napoleon, nor even the "Irish Sketch Book," do much to make their writer known. It was his "Vanity Fair," which issued in shilling monthly parts, took the world of readers, as it were, by storm; and an appreciative article, from the hand of a friend, in the "Edinburgh Review" in 1848, which, for the first time, helped to spread the tidings of a new master of fiction among us, destined to make a name second to none in English literature in its own field.

A leading article in a morning newspaper on the occasion of Mr. Thackeray's death, in telling the anecdote of his offer to illustrate "Pickwick," adds, that disappointed at the rejection of his offer, he exclaimed, "Well, if you will not let me draw, I will write;" and from that hour determined to compete with his illustrious brother novelist for public favour. Nothing could be more opposed to the facts than this coloured version of the anecdote. It was not for a year or two after the event referred to that he began seriously to devote himself to literary labour; and his articles, published anonymously, and only now for the first time brought into notice, became recognised from their *noms de plume*, to have been written by him, contain the best evidences that he felt no shadow of ill-will for a rejection which he always good-humouredly alluded to as "Mr. Pickwick's lucky escape." He was an early and sincere admirer of Mr. Dickens's writings. In the midst of the often savagely sarcastic reviews of literature which he contributed to home and American magazines, there are frequent references—generally enthusiastic; and even when taking exception to some feature of the work, always respectful to the great powers of the man whom the readers of a subsequent period delighted to contrast with himself as the only living writer of fiction worthy to be named with the author of "Vanity Fair." In the magazine for February 1840, at the end of a clever satire upon the "Newgate Calendar" school of romance, purporting to be written by Ikey Solomons, jun., he thus remarks upon "Oliver Twist:"—"No man has read that remarkable tale without being interested in poor Nancy and her murderer, and especially amused and tickled by the gambols of the skilful Dodger and his companions. The power of the writer is so amazing that the reader at once becomes his captive, and must follow him whithersoever he leads; and to what are we led? Breathless to watch all the crimes of Fagin, tenderly to deplore the errors of Nancy, to have for Bill Sikes a kind of pity and admiration, and an absolute love for the society of the Dodger. All these heroes stepped from the novel on to the stage; and the whole London public, from peers to chimney-sweeps, were interested about a set of ruffians whose occupations are thievery, murder, and prostitution. A most agreeable set of rascals, indeed, who have their virtues, too, but not good company for any man. We had better pass them by in decent silence; for, as no writer can or dare tell the *whole* truth concerning them, and faithfully explain their vices, there is no need to give *ex-parte* statements of their virtues.   *   *   *   *   *

The pathos of the workhouse scenes in 'Oliver Twist,' of the Fleet Prison descriptions in 'Pickwick,' is genuine and pure—as much of this as you please; as tender a hand to the poor, as kindly a word to the unhappy, as you will; but, in the name of common sense, let us not expend our sympathies on cutthroats, and other such prodigies of evil!"

Still later, when commenting on the Royal Academy Exhibition, we find another interesting reference to Mr. Dickens, with a prophecy of his future greatness:—" Look, (he says in the assumed character of Michael Angelo Titmarsh), at the portrait of Mr. Dickens,—well arranged as a picture, good in colour, and light and shadow, and as a likeness perfectly amazing; a looking-glass could not render a better facsimile. Here we have the real identical man Dickens: the artist must have understood the inward Boz as well as the outward before he made this admirable representation of him. What cheerful intelligence there is about the man's eyes and large forehead! The mouth is too large and full, too eager and active, perhaps; the smile is very sweet and generous. If Monsieur de Balzac, that voluminous physiognomist, could examine this head, he would, no doubt, interpret every tone and wrinkle in it: the nose firm, and well placed; the nostrils wide and full, as are the nostrils of all men of genius (this is Monsieur Balzac's maxim). The past and the future, says Jean Paul, are written in every countenance. I think we may promise ourselves a brilliant future from this one. There seems no flagging as yet in it, no sense of fatigue, or consciousness of decaying power. Long mayest thou, O Boz! reign over thy comic kingdom; long may we pay tribute, whether of threepence weekly or of a shilling monthly, it matters not. Mighty prince! at thy imperial feet, Titmarsh, humblest of thy servants, offers his vows of loyalty and his humble tribute of praise."

But a still more touching and beautiful tribute to Mr. Dickens's genius from the yet unknown Michael Angelo Titmarsh appears in "Fraser" for July 1844. A box of Christmas books is supposed to have been sent by the editor to Titmarsh in his retirement in Switzerland, whence the latter writes his notions of their contents. The last book of all is Mr. Dickens's Christmas Carol—we mean the story of old Scrooge—the immortal precursor of that long line of Christmas stories which are now so familiar to his readers.

"And now (says the critic) there is but one book left in the box, the smallest one, but oh! how much the best of all. It is the work of the master of all the English humourists now alive; the young man who came and took his place calmly at the head of the whole tribe, and who has kept it. Think of all we owe Mr. Dickens since those half dozen years, that store of happy hours that he has made us pass, the kindly and pleasant companions whom he has introduced to us; the harmless laughter, the generous wit, the frank, manly, human love which he has taught us to feel! Every month of those years has brought us some kind token from this delightful genius. His books may have lost in art, perhaps, but could we afford to wait? Since the days when the 'Spectator' was produced by a man of kindred mind and temper, what books have appeared that have taken so affectionate a hold of the English public as these?

* * * * *

Who can listen to objections regarding such a book as this? It seems to me a national benefit, and to every man or woman who reads it a personal kindness. The last two people I heard speak of it were women; neither knew the other, or the author, and both said, by way of criticism, 'God bless him!' * * * * *
As for TINY TIM, there is a certain passage in the book regarding that young gentleman, about which a man should hardly venture to speak in print or in public, any more than he would of any other affections of his private heart. There is not a reader in England but that little creature will be a bond of union between author and him; and he will say of Charles Dickens, as the woman just now, 'God bless him!' What a feeling is this for a writer to be able to inspire, and what a reward to reap."

Mr. Thackeray was in Paris in March, 1836, at the time of the execution of Fieschi and

Lacenaire, upon which subject he wrote some remarks in one of his anonymous papers, which it is interesting to compare with the more advanced views in favour of the abolition of the punishment of death, which are familiar to the readers of his subsequent article, "On going to see a Man Hanged." He did not witness the execution either of Fieschi or Lacenaire, though he made unsuccessful attempts to be present at both cases.

"The day for Fieschi's death was, purposely, kept secret; and he was executed at a remote quarter of the town." But the scene on the morning when his execution did not take place was never forgotten by the young English artist.

It was carnival time, and the rumour had pretty generally been carried abroad, that the culprit was to die on that morning. A friend, who accompanied Thackeray, came many miles, through the mud and dark, in order to be "in at the death." They set out before light, floundering through the muddy Champs Elysées, where were many others bent upon the same errand. They passed by the

Concert of Musard, then held in the Rue St. Honoré; and round this, in the wet, a number of coaches were collected; the ball was just up; and a crowd of people, in hideous masquerade, drunk, tired, dirty, dressed in horrible old frippery, and daubed with filthy rouge, were trooping out of the place; tipsy women and men, shrieking, jabbering, gesticulating, as French will do; parties swaggering, staggering forwards, arm in arm, reeling to and fro across the street, and yelling songs in chorus. Hundreds of these were bound for the show, and the two friends thought themselves lucky in finding a vehicle to the execution place, at the Barriere d'Enfer. As they crossed the river, and entered the Rue d'Enfer, crowds of students, black workmen, and more drunken devils, from more carnival balls, were filling it; and on the grand place there were thousands of these assembled, looking out for Fieschi and his *cortége*. They waited, but no throat-cutting that morning; no august spectacle of satisfied justice; and the eager spectators were obliged to return, disappointed of their expected breakfast of blood. " It would " (says Thackeray) " have been a fine scene, that execution, could it but have taken place in the midst of the mad mountebanks and tipsy strumpets, who had flocked so far to witness it, wishing to wind up the delights of their carnival by a *bonne-bouche* of a murder."

The other attempt was equally unfortunate. The same friend accompanied him; but they arrived too late on the ground to be present at the execution of Lacenaire and his co-mate in murder, Avril. But as they came to the spot (a gloomy round space, within the barrier—three roads led to it—and, outside, they saw the wine-shops and restaurateurs of the barrier looking gay and inviting), they only found, in the midst of it, a little pool of ice, just partially tinged with red. Two or three idle street boys were dancing and stamping about this pool; and when the Englishmen asked one of them whether the execution had taken place, he began dancing more madly than ever, and shrieked out with a loud fantastic theatrical voice, " *Venez tous Messieurs et Dames, voyez ici le sang du monstre, Lacénaire, et de son compagnon, le traitre Avril;* " and, straightway, all the other gamins screamed out the words in chorus, and took hands and danced round the little puddle. "Oh, august Justice!" exclaimed the young art-student, "your meal was followed by a pretty appropriate grace! Was any man who saw the show deterred, or frightened, or moralized in any way? He had gratified his appetite for blood, and this was all. Remark what a good breakfast you eat after an execution; how pleasant it is to cut jokes after it, and upon it. This merry, pleasant mood, is brought on by the blood-tonic."

Mr. Thackeray returned to London in March, 1836, and resided for a few months in the house of his stepfather, Major Henry Carmichael Smyth. The principal object of his return was to concert with Major Smyth, who was a gentleman of some literary attainments, a project for starting a daily newspaper. The time was believed to be remarkably opportune for the new journal; the old oppressive newspaper stamp being about to be repealed, and a penny stamp, giving the privilege of a free transition through the post, about to be substituted. The project was to form a small joint-stock company, to be called the

Metropolitan Newspaper Company, with a capital of 60,000*l*., in shares of 10*l*. each. The Major, as chief proprietor, became chairman of the new company; Laman Blanchard was appointed editor, Douglas Jerrold a dramatic critic, and Thackeray the Paris correspondent. An old and respectable, though decayed journal, entitled the *Public Ledger*, was purchased by the company; and on the 15th of September, the first day of the new stamp duty, the newspaper was started, with the title of the *Constitutional and Public Ledger*. The politics of the paper were ultra-liberal. Its programme was entire freedom of the press, extension of popular suffrage, vote by ballot, shortening of duration of parliaments, equality of civil rights and religious liberty, &c. A number of the most eminent of the advanced party, including Mr. Grote, Sir William Molesworth, Mr. Joseph Hume, and Colonel Thompson, publicly advertised their intention to support the new journal, and to promote its circulation. Mr. Thackeray's Paris letters, signed "S. T.," commenced on the 24th of September, and were continued at intervals until the Spring of the following year: they present little worth notice. At that time the chatty correspondent, who discourses upon all things save the subject of his letter, was a thing unknown. Bare facts, such as the telegraph-wires now bring us, with here and there a *soupçon* of philosophical reflection, was the utmost that the readers of newspapers in those days demanded of the useful individual who kept watch in the capital of civilization for events of interest. Generally, however, the letters are characterized by a strong distaste for the Government of July, and by an ardent liberalism which had but slightly cooled down when, at the Oxford election in 1857, he declared himself an uncompromising advocate of vote by ballot. Writing from Paris on October 8, he says:—" We are luckily too strong to dread much from open hostility, or to be bullied back into toryism by our neighbours; but if radicalism be a sin in their eyes, it exists, thank God! not merely across the Alps, but across the channel." The new journal, however, was far from prosperous. After enlarging its size and raising its price from fourpence-halfpenny to fivepence, it gradually declined in circulation.

The last number appeared on the 1st of July, 1837, bearing black borders for the death of the king. " We can estimate, therefore (says the dying speech of the *Constitutional*), the feelings of the gentleman who once walked at his own funeral," and the editor, or perhaps his late Paris Correspondent adds, " The adverse circumstances have been various. In the philosophy of ill-luck it may be laid down as a principle that every point of discouragement tends to one common centre of defeat. When the fates do concur in one discomfiture their unanimity is wonderful. So has it happened in the case of the *Constitutional*. In the first place, a delay of some months consequent upon the postponement of the newspaper stamp reduction, operated on the minds of many who were originally parties to the enterprise; in the next, the majority of those who remained faithful were wholly inexperienced in the art and mystery of the practical working of an important daily journal; in the third, and consequent upon the other two, there was the want of those abundant means, and of that wise application of resources, without which no efficient organ of the interests of any class of men—to say nothing of the interests of that first and greatest class whose welfare has been our dearest aim, and most constant object—can be successfully established. Then came further misgivings on the part of friends, and the delusive undertakings of friends in disguise." The venture proved in every way a disastrous one. Although nominally supported by a joint-stock company, the burden of the undertaking really rested upon the original promoters, of whom Major Smyth was the principal, while his stepson, Mr. Thackeray, also lost nearly all that remained of his fortune.

It was shortly after the failure of the *Constitutional* that Mr. Thackeray married in Paris a Miss Shaw, sister of the Captain Shaw, an Indian officer, who was one of the mourners at his funeral, an Irish lady of good family, who bore him two daughters, the elder of whom has recently shown something of her illustrious father's talent, in the remarkable story of "Elizabeth," written by her, and published in the "Cornhill Magazine." In 1837 he left that city with his family, and resided for two years in London, when for the first time he began to devote himself seriously to literary labour, adding, according to a French writer, occasional work as an illustrator. We are told that he contributed some papers to the *Times* during Barnes's editorship—an article on "Fielding" among them. He is believed to have been connected with two literary papers of his time— the *Torch*, edited by Felix Fax, Esq., and the *Parthenon*, which must not be confounded with a literary journal with the same name recently existing. The *Torch*, which was started on the 26th of August, 1837, ran only for six months; and was immediately succeeded by the *Parthenon*, which had a longer existence. In neither paper, however, is it possible to trace any sign of that shrewd criticism or overflowing humour which distinguish the papers in "Fraser." For the latter publication he laboured assiduously, and it was at this time that the "Yellowplush Papers" appeared, with occasional notices of the Exhibitions of Paintings in London. Among his writings of this period (1837–1840), we also find "Stubb's Calendar, or the Fatal Boots," contributed to his friend Cruikshank's "Comic Almanac" for 1839, and since included in the "Miscellanies;" "Catherine, by Ikey Solomons, jun.," a long continuous story, founded on the crime of Catherine Hays, the celebrated murderess of the last century, and intended to ridicule the novels of the school of Jack Sheppard; "Cartouche" and "Painsonnet," two stories, and "Epistles to the Liberator." In 1839 he visited Paris again at the request of the proprietor of "Fraser," in order to write an account of the French Exhibition of Paintings, which appears in the December number.

On his return he devoted himself to the writing of "The Shabby Genteel" story, which was begun in "Fraser" for June, and continued in the numbers for July, August, and October, when it stopped unfinished at the ninth chapter. The story of this strange failure is a mournful one. While busily engaged in writing this beautiful and affecting story, a dark shadow descended upon his household, making all the associations of that time painful to him forever. The terrible truth, long suspected, that the chosen partner of his good and evil fortunes could never participate in the success for which he had toiled, became confirmed.

The mental disease which had attacked his wife rapidly developed itself, until the hopes which had sustained those to whom she was most dear were wholly extinguished. Mr. Thackeray was not one of those who love to parade their domestic sorrows before the world. No explanation of his strange failure to complete his story was given to his readers; but, years afterwards, in reprinting it in his miscellanies, he alluded to the circumstances which had paralyzed his hand, and rendered him incapable of ever resuming the thread of his story, with a touching suggestiveness for those who knew the facts. The tale was interrupted, he said, " at a sad period of the writer's own life." When the republication of the miscellanies was announced, it was his intention to complete the little story— but the colours were long since dry—the artist's hand had changed. It " was best," he says, " to leave the sketch as it was when first resigned seventeen years ago. The memory of the past is renewed as he looks at it."*

It was in 1840 that Mr. Thackeray contributed to the "Westminster" a beautiful and appreciative

* Miscellanies," vol. iv. p. 324.

article upon the productions of his friend, George Cruikshank, illustrated—an unusual thing for the great organ of the philosophers of the schools of Bentham, J. Mill, and Sir W. Molesworth—with numerous specimens of the comic sketches of the subject of the papers. His defence of Cruikshank from the cavils of those who loved to dwell upon his defects as a draughtsman is full of sound criticism; his claim for his friend as something far greater, a man endowed with that rarest of all faculties, the power to create, are inspired by a generous enthusiasm which give a life and spirit to the paper not often found in a critical review. But perhaps the finest passage in the article is the concluding words:—" Many artists, we hear, hold his works rather cheap; they prate about bad drawing, want of scientific knowledge—they would have something vastly more neat, regular, anatomical. Not one of the whole band, most likely, but can paint an academy figure better than himself—nay, or a portrait of an alderman's lady and family of children. But look down the list of the painters, and tell us who are they? How many among these men are poets, makers, possessing the faculty to create, the greatest among the gifts with which Providence has endowed the mind of man? Say how many there are? Count up what they have done, and see what, in the course of some nine and twenty years, has been done by this indefatigable man. What amazing energetic fecundity do we find in him! As a boy, he began to fight for bread, has been hungry (twice a day, we trust) ever since, and has been obliged to sell his wit for his bread week by week. And his wit, sterling gold as it is, will find no such purchasers as the fashionable painter's thin pinchbeck, who can live comfortably for six weeks, when paid for and painting a portrait, and fancies his mind prodigiously occupied all the while. There was an artist in Paris—an artist hairdresser—who used to be fatigued and take restoratives after inventing a new coiffure. By no such gentle operation of head-dressing has Cruikshank lived; time was (we are told so in print) when for a picture with thirty heads in it, he was paid three guineas—a poor week's pittance truly, and a dire week's labour. We make no doubt that the same labour would at present bring him twenty times the sum; but whether it be ill-paid or well, what labour has Mr. Cruikshank's been! Week by week, for thirty years, to produce something new; some smiling offspring of painful labour, quite independent and distinct from its ten thousand jovial brethren; in what hours of sorrow and ill-health to be told by the world, 'Make us laugh, or you starve—give us fresh fun; we have eaten up the old, and are hungry.' And all this has he been obliged to do —to wring laughter day by day, sometimes, perhaps, out of want, often, certainly, from ill-health and depression—to keep the fire of his brain perpetually alight, for the greedy public will give it no leisure to cool. This he has done, and done well. He has told a thousand new truths in as many strange and fascinating ways; he has given a thousand new and pleasant thoughts to millions of people; he has never used his wit dishonestly; he has never, in all the exuberance of his frolicsome nature, caused a single painful or guilty blush. How little do we think of the extraordinary power of this man, and how ungrateful are we to him!" This long paper, signed with the Greek letter Theta, is little known; but

Mr. Thackeray frequently referred to it as a labour in which he had felt a peculiar pleasure.

In a private letter to a literary friend, written in 1850, he says :—Don't forget the copy of C's Almanack. There is one print of a wedding party, which, if it amuses you as it has amused me, will be worth the price and carriage. When you get it, note the gruff old gentleman on the right, who has screwed up his face with a firm resolve that *he* will not shed tears with the rest of the company. I fancy that he is a monied man, and that there have been family 'expectations' from him. Something seems wanting about his head. Can it be a pen behind the ear? And now I think of it, those features have a bill-discounting expression, and he has been accustomed to say 'no; couldn't entertain it!'"*

In the summer of 1840 he collected some of his sketches inserted in "Fraser," and other periodicals, English and foreign, and republished them under the title of "The Paris Sketch Book." This work is interesting as the first indepen-

* The author has been fortunate in obtaining permission to insert a copy of the picture referred to.

dent publication of the author, but of its contents few things are now remembered. The dedicatory letter prefixed, however, is peculiarly characteristic of the writer. It relates to a circumstance which had occurred to him some time previously in Paris. The old days when money was abundant, and loitering among the pictures of the Paris galleries could be indulged in without remorse had gone. The *res angusta domi* with which genius has so often been disturbed in its day-dreams began to be familiar to him. The unfortunate failure of the *Constitutional*,—a loss which he, years afterwards, occasionally referred to as a foolish commercial speculation on which he had ventured in his youth, had absorbed the whole of his patrimony. At such a time a temporary difficulty in meeting a creditor's demand was not uncommon. On one such occasion, a M. Aretz, a tailor in the Rue Richelieu, who had for some time supplied him with coats and trousers, presented him with a small account for those articles, and was met with a statement from his debtor that an immediate settlement of the bill would be extremely inconvenient to him. To his astonishment the reply of the creditor was, "Mon Dieu, Sir, let not that annoy you. If you want money, as a gentleman often does in a strange country, I have a thousand franc note at my house which is quite at your service." The generous offer was accepted. The coin which, in proof of the tailor's esteem for his customer, was advanced without any interest, was duly repaid together with the account; but the circumstance could not be forgotten. His debtor felt how becoming it was to acknowledge, and praise virtue, as he slyly said, wherever he might find it, and to point it out for the admiration and example of his fellow-men. Accordingly, he determined to dedicate his first book to the generous tailor, giving at full length his name and address. In the dedicatory letter, he accordingly alludes to this anecdote, adding—

"History or experience, sir, makes us acquainted with so few actions that can be compared to yours; a kindness like yours, from a stranger and a tailor, seems to me so astonishing, that you must pardon me for thus making your virtue public, and acquainting the English nation with your merit and your name. Let me add, sir, that you live on the first floor; that your clothes and fit are excellent, and your charges moderate and just; and, as an humble tribute of my admiration, permit me to lay these volumes at your feet.

"Your obliged, faithful Servant,
"M. A. TITMARSH."

A second edition of the "Paris Sketch Book" was announced by the publisher, Macrone—the same publisher who had a few years before given to the world the "Sketches by Boz," the first of Mr. Dickens' publications; but the second edition was probably only one of those conventional fictions with which the spirits of young authors are sustained. Though containing many flashes of the Titmarsh humour, many eloquent passages, and much interesting reading of a light kind, the public took but a passing interest in it. Years after, in quoting its title, the author good-humouredly remarked, in a parenthesis, that some copies, he believed, might still be found unsold at the publisher's; but the book was forgotten and most of its contents were rejected by the writer when preparing his selected miscellanies for the press. A similar couple of volumes published by

Cunningham in 1841, under the title of "Comic Tales and Sketches, edited and illustrated by Mr. Michael Angelo Titmarsh," and an independent republication, also in two volumes, of the "Yellowplush Papers," from "Fraser," were somewhat more successful. The former contained "Major Gahagan," and "The Bedford-row Conspiracy," reprinted from "The New Monthly," "Stubbs's Calendar, or the Fatal Boots," from Cruikshank's "Comic Almanack;" some amusing criticisms on the "Sea Captain," and "Lady Charlotte Bury's Diary," and other papers from "Fraser." The illustrations to the volumes were tinted etchings of a somewhat more careful character than those unfinished artistic drolleries in which he generally indulged.

In Dec. 1840, he again visited Paris, and remained there until the summer of the following year. He was in that city on the memorable occasion of the second funeral of Napoleon, or the ceremony of conveying the remains of that great warrior, of whom, as a child, he had obtained a living glimpse, to their last resting place at the *Hôtel des Invalides*. An account of that ceremony in the form of a letter to Miss Smith, was published by Macrone. It was a small square pamphlet, chiefly memorable now as containing at the end his remarkable poem of "The Chronicle of the Drum." About this time he advertised as preparing for immediate publication, a book entitled "Dinner Reminiscences, or the Young Gormandiser's Guide at Paris, by Mr. M. A. Titmarsh." It was to be issued by Hugh Cunningham, the publisher of St. Martin's place, Trafalgar-square; but we believe, was never published.

It was in the September number of "Fraser," for 1841, that he commenced his story of the "History of Samuel Titmarsh, and the Great Hoggarty Diamond," which though it failed to achieve an extraordinary popularity, first convinced that select few who judge for themselves in matters of literature and art, of the great power and promise of the unknown "Titmarsh." Mr. Carlyle, in his "Life of John Sterling," quotes the following remarkable passage from a letter of the latter to his mother, written at this period :—" I have seen no new books, but am reading your last. I got hold of the two first

numbers of the 'Hoggarty Diamond,' and read them with extreme delight. What is there better in Fielding or Goldsmith? The man is a true genius, and with quiet and comfort might produce masterpieces that would last as long as any we have, and delight millions of unborn readers. There is more truth and nature in one of these papers than in all ——'s novels put together."
"Thackeray (adds Mr. Carlyle), always a close friend of the Sterling house, will observe that this is dated 1841, not 1851, and will have his own reflections on the matter." The "Hoggarty Diamond" was continued in the numbers for October and November, and completed in December, 1841. In the number for June of the following year, " Fitzboodle's Confessions " were commenced, and were continued at intervals down to the end of 1843. The " Irish Sketch Book," in two volumes, detailing an Irish tour, was also published in the latter year. The " Sketch Book," did not at the time attract much attention. The " Luck of Barry Lyndon," by many considered the most original of his writings, was begun and finished at No. 88, St. James-street, previously known

as the Conservative Club, where at this time he occupied chambers. The first part appeared in "Fraser," for January, 1844, and was continued regularly every month, till its completion in the December number. He was engaged a short time before this as assistant editor of the *Examiner* newspaper, to which journal he contributed numerous articles; and among his papers in " Fraser," and other magazines of the same period, we find, "Memorials of Gormandising;" "Pictorial Rhapsodies on the Exhibitions of Paintings;" "Bluebeard's Ghost;" a satirical article on Grant's "Paris and the Parisians;" a "Review of a Box of Novels," (already quoted from); "Little Travels and Roadside Sketches," (chiefly in Belgium); "The *Partie Fine*, by Lancelot Wagstaff;" a comic story with a sequel entitled "Arabella, or the Moral of the *Partie Fine*;" "Carmen Lilliense;" "Picture Gossip;" more comic sketches, with the titles of "The chest of Cigars, by Lancelot Wagstaff;" "Bob Robinson's First Love;" and "Barmecside Banquets," and an admirable satirical review entitled "A Gossip about Christmas Books."

The "Carmen Lilliense" will be well remembered by the readers of the "Miscellanies," published in 1857, in which it was included. Mr. Thackeray was in the north of France and in Belgium about the period when it is dated (2nd September, 1843); and the ballad describes a real accident which befell him, though doubtless somewhat heightened in effect. It tells how leaving Paris, with only twenty pounds in his pocket, for a trip in Belgium, he arrived at Antwerp, where feeling for his purse, he found it had vanished with the entire amount of his little treasure. Some rascal on the road had picked his pocket; and nothing was left but to borrow ten guineas of a friend whom he met, and to write a note to England addressed to " Grandmamma," for whom we may probably read some other member of the Titmarsh family. The ten guineas, however, were soon gone, and the sensitive Titmarsh found himself in a position of great delicacy. What was to be done? "To stealing," says the ballad, " he could never come." To pawn his watch he felt himself " too genteel;" besides, he had left his watch at home, which at once put an end to any debates on this point. There was nothing to do but to wait for the remittance, and beguile the time with a poetical description of his woes. The guests around him ask for their bills. Titmarsh is in agonies. The landlord regards him as a "Lord-Anglais," serves him with the best of meat and drink, and is proud of his patronage. A sense of being a kind of impostor weighs upon him. The landlord's eye becomes painful to look at. Opposite is a dismal building—the prison-house of Lille, where, by a summary process, familiar to French law, foreigners who run in debt without the means of paying may be lodged. He is almost tempted to go into the old Flemish church and invoke the saints there after the fashion of the country. One of their pictures on the walls becomes, in his imagination, like the picture of "Grandmamma," with a smile upon its countenance. Delightful dream! and one of good omen. He returns to his hotel, and there to his relief, finds the long-expected letter, in the well-known hand, addressed to "Mr. M. A. Titmarsh, Lille." He obtains the means of redeeming his credit, bids farewell to his host without any exposure, takes the diligence, and is restored to his home that evening. Such are the humourous exaggerations with which he depicts his temporary troubles at Lille, in the shape of a ballad, originally intended, we believe, for the amusement of his family, but finally inserted in " Fraser."

It was in July, 1844, that Mr. Thackeray started on a tour in the East—the result of a hasty invitation, and of a present of a free pass from a friend connected with the Peninsular and Oriental Steam Navigation Company. His sudden departure, upon less than thirty-six hours notice, is pleasantly detailed in the preface to his book, published at Christmas, 1845, with the title of " Notes of a Journey from Cornhill to Grand Cairo by way of Lisbon, Athens, Constantinople, and Jerusalem: performed in the steamers of the Peninsular and Oriental Company. By M. A. Titmarsh, author of The Irish Sketch-book," &c.

The book was illustrated with coloured drawings by the author, treating, in a not exaggerated vein of fun, the peculiarities of the daily life of the East. The little book was well received, and in the reviews of it there is evidence of the growing interest of the public in the writer. For the first time it presented him to his readers in his true name, for though the "Titmarsh" fiction is preserved on the title page, the prefatory matter is signed " W. M. Thackeray."

"'Who is Titmarsh?' says one of his critics at this time. Such is the ejaculatory formula in which public curiosity gives vent to its ignorant impatience of pseudononymous renown. 'Who is Michael Angelo Titmarsh?' Such is the note of interrogation which has been heard at intervals these several seasons back, among groups of elderly loungers in that row of clubs, Pall-mall; from fairy lips, as the light wheels whirled along the row called ' Rotten,' and oft amid keen-eyed men in that grand father of rows, which the children of literature call Paternoster. * * *

" This problem has been variously and conflictingly solved, as in the parallel case of the grim, old, *stat nominis umbra*. There is a hint in both instances of some mysterious connexion with the remote regions of Bengal, and an erect old pigtail of the E.I.C.S., boasts in the 'horizontal' jungle off Hanover-square, of having had the dubious advantage of his personal acquaintanceship in Upper India, where his I O U's were signed Major Goliah Gahagan; and several specimens of that documentary character, in good preservation, he offers at a low figure to amateurs."

The foundation in 1841 of a weekly periodical, serving as a vehicle for the circulation of the lighter papers of humourists, had had unquestionably an important influence in the development of his talents and fame. From an early date he was connected with "Punch," at first as the "Fat Contributor," and soon after as the author of 'Jeames's Diary," and "The Snob Papers." If satire could do aught to check the pride of the vulgar upstart, or shame social hypocrisy into truth and simplicity, these writings would accomplish the task. In fact Thackeray's name was now becoming known, and people began to distinguish and inquire for his contributions; his illustrations in " Punch " being as funny as his articles were. The series called " Jeames's Diary " caused great amusement and no little flutter in high polite circles, for the deposition from the throne of railwaydom of the famous original of "Jeames de la Pluche" had hardly then begun, though it was probably accelerated by the universal titters of recognition which welcomed the weekly accounts of the changing fortunes of "Jeames."

The great work, however, which was to stamp the name of Thackeray for ever in the minds of English readers was yet to come. Hitherto all his writings had been brief and desultory; but in contributing to magazines his style had gradually matured itself. That ease of expression, and that repose which seems so full of power, were never more exemplified than in some of his latest essays in "Fraser," before book writing had absorbed all his time. His article on Sir E. B. Lytton's "Memoir of Laman Blanchard," his paper "On Illustrated Children's Books," his satirical proposal to Mons. Alexandre Dumas for a continuation of "Ivanhoe," all contributed to "Fraser" in 1846, and his article—we believe the last which he wrote for that periodical, entitled "A Grumble about Christmas Books," published in January, 1847, are equal to anything in his later works. The first-mentioned of these papers, indeed—the remonstrance with Laman Blanchard's biographer is unsurpassed for the eloquence of its defence of the calling of men of letters, and for the tenderness and manly simplicity with which it touches on the history of the unfortunate subject of the memoir.

"Mrs. Perkins's Ball," a Christmas Book, was published in December, 1846. But its author had long been preparing for a more serious undertaking; some time before, he had sketched some chapters entitled "Pencil Sketches of English Society," which he had offered to the late Mr. Colburn for insertion in the "New Monthly Magazine." It formed a portion of a continuous story, of a length not yet determined, and was rejected by Mr. Colburn after consideration. The papers which Mr. Thackeray had contributed to the "New Monthly" were chiefly slight comic stories—perhaps the least favourable specimens of his powers. They were, indeed, not inferior to the common run of magazine papers, and were certainly not equal to his contributions to "Fraser." In fact, as a contributor to the "New

Monthly," he had achieved no remarkable success, and his papers appear to have been little in demand there. Whether the manuscript had been offered to "Fraser"—the magazine in which "Titmarsh" had secured popularity, and where he was certainly more at home, we cannot say. Happily, the author of " Pencil Sketches of English Society," though suspending his projected work, did not abandon it. He saw in its opening chapters—certainly not the best portions of the story when completed—the foundations of a work which was to secure him at last a fame among contemporary writers in his own proper name. The success of Mr. Dickens's shilling monthly parts suggested to him to make it the commencement of a substantive work of fiction, to be published month by month, with illustrations by the author. The work grew up by degrees, and finally took shape under the better title of "Vanity Fair." It was during this time, the latter part of 1846, that he removed to his house, at No. 13, Young-street, Kensington, a favourite locality with him, in which house he resided for some years. He also at this time occupied chambers at

No. 10, Crown-office-row, Temple, the comfortable retirement in which " up four pair of stairs, with its grand view, when the sun was shining, of the chimney-pots over the way," he has himself described. His friend, Mr. Tom Taylor, the well-known dramatist and biographer, had chambers in the same house; and we believe, on the demolition of No. 10, Crown-office-row, wrote a poem, published in the pages of " Punch," in which, if we remember rightly, mention is made of the fact of Thackeray's having resided there. Mr. Thackeray was called to the bar by the Hon. Society of the Middle Temple, in 1848, though he never practised, and never probably intended to do so. The Benchers, however, were not insensible to the addition to the numerous literary associations with their venerable and quiet retreat which they thus gained. After his death, there was some proposition to bury him in the Temple, of which he was a member, amid

> Those bricky towers
> The which on Thames' broad back do ride
> Where now the student lawyers have their bowers,
> Where whilom wont the Templar Knights to bide,
> Till they decayed through pride.

There Goldsmith is buried, and Thackeray's ashes

would have been fitly laid near those of the author of the " Vicar of Wakefield," whose brilliant genius he so heartily eulogised, and whose many shortcomings he so tenderly touched upon in the " Lectures on the Humourists." But, after consultation with his family it was deemed better that he should rest with his own people in Kensal Green. Pending this decision, the sanction of the Benchers to interment within the precincts of the Temple Church had been asked and cheerfully accorded, and when the Kensal Green Cemetery was finally decided upon, the Benchers were requested to permit the erection of a memorial slab in their church. Their reply to this was, that not only should they be honoured by such a memento, but that, if allowed, they would have it erected at their own cost.*

* Letter of Mr. Edmund Yates in the *Belfast Whig*.

CHAPTER IV.

VANITY FAIR—FIRST MONTHLY NUMBER—NOTICES OF THE EDINBURGH REVIEW—A LITTLE CHRISTMAS BOOK—LETTER ON THE DIGNITY OF LITERATURE—ANNOYED BY ADVERSE CRITICISM—NOTICE OF THE TIMES CRITIQUE—BEGINS TO DELIVER LECTURES—HIS SUCCESS—LECTURES IN AMERICA—HIS SUCCESS—NOTICES OF NEWSPAPERS—PREFACE TO AN AMERICAN EDITION OF HIS WORKS—PUBLICATION OF HENRY ESMOND—INCIDENT IN CONNEXION WITH THE PUBLICATION OF THE NEWCOMES—SECOND JOURNEY TO THE UNITED STATES—LECTURES ON THE "GEORGES"—ADDRESS TO THE ELECTORS OF OXFORD—THE ELECTION—THACKERAY AND DICKENS—CORRESPONDENCE.

The first monthly portion of "Vanity Fair" was published on the 1st of February, 1847, in the yellow wrapper which served to distinguish it from Mr. Dickens's stories, and which afterwards became the standard colour for the monthly wrappers of Mr. Thackeray's stories. The work was continued monthly, and finished with the number for July of the following year. The friends of Mr. Thackeray, and all those who had watched his career with special interest, saw in it at once a work of greater promise than any that had appeared since the dawn of Mr. Dickens's fame; but the critical journals received it somewhat coldly. One of the most influential of these journals, in the first numbers, perhaps, indicates best the tone of its reception at this early period.

It is generally acknowledged that, to the thoughtful and appreciative article in the "Edinburgh Review" of January, 1848, reviewing the first eleven numbers of the work only, is due the merit of first authoritatively calling attention to the great power it displayed. The writer was evidently one who knew Mr. Thackeray well; for he gives a sketch of his life, and mentions having met him some years before painting in the Louvre in Paris. "In forming (says this judicious writer) our general estimate of this writer, we wish to be understood as referring principally, if not exclusively, to 'Vanity Fair' (a novel in monthly parts), though still unfinished; so immeasurably superior, in our opinion, is this to every other known production of his pen. The great charm of this work is its entire freedom from mannerism and affectation both in style and sentiment—the confiding frankness with which the reader is addressed—the thoroughbred carelessness with which the author permits the thoughts and feelings suggested by the situations to flow in their natural channel, as if conscious that nothing mean or unworthy, nothing requiring to be shaded, gilded, or dressed up in company attire, could fall from him. In a word, the book is the work of a gentleman, which is one great merit; and not the work of a fine (or would-be fine) gentleman, which is another. Then, again, he never exhausts, elaborates, or insists too much upon anything; he drops his finest remarks and happiest illustrations as Buckingham dropped his pearls, and leaves them to be picked up and appreciated as chance may bring a discriminating observer to the spot. His effects are uniformly the effects of sound, wholesome, legitimate art; and we need hardly add, that we are never harrowed up with physical horrors of the Eugene Sue school in his writings, or that there are no melodramatic villains to be found in them. One touch of nature makes the whole world kin, and here are touches of nature by the dozen. His pathos (though not so deep as Mr. Dickens') is exquisite; the more so, perhaps, because he seems to struggle against it, and to be half ashamed of being caught in the melting mood; but the attempt to be caustic, satirical, ironical, or philosophical, on such occasions, is uniformly vain; and again and again have we found reason to admire how an originally fine and kind nature remains essentially free from worldliness, and, in the highest pride of intellect, pays homage to the heart."

It was at this time that his friend Mr. Hannay tells us that he first had the pleasure of seeing him. "'Vanity Fair,'" he adds, "was then unfinished, but its success was made; and he spoke frankly and genially of his work and his career. 'Vanity Fair,' always, we think, ranked in his own mind as best in story of his greater books; and he once pointed out to us the very house in Russell-square where his imaginary Sedleys lived—a curious proof of the reality his creations had for his mind." The same writer tells us that when he congratulated him, many years ago, on the touch in "Vanity Fair" in which Becky admires her husband when he is giving Lord Steyne the chastisement which ruins *her* for life, the author answered with that fervour as well as heartiness of frankness which distinguished him:—"Well, when I wrote the sentence, I slapped my fist on the table, and said, 'That is a touch of genius!'" "Vanity Fair" soon afterwards rose rapidly in public favour, and a new work from the pen of its author was eagerly looked for.

During the time of publication of "Vanity Fair" he had found time to write and publish the little Christmas book entitled "Our Street," which appeared in December, 1847, and reached a second edition soon after Christmas. "Vanity Fair" was followed in 1849 with another long work of fiction, entitled the "History of Pendennis; his Fortunes and Misfortunes, his Friends and his Greatest Enemy; with Illustrations by the Author;" which was completed in two volumes. In this year, too, he published "Dr. Birch" and "Rebecca and Rowena." It was during the publication of "Pendennis" that a criticism in the *Morning Chronicle* and in the *Examiner* newspapers drew from him the following remarkable letter on the "Dignity of Literature," addressed to the Editor of the latter journal:—

"*Reform Club, Jan. 8th*, 1850.

"To the Editor of the *Morning Chronicle*.

"SIR,—In a leading article of your journal of Thursday the 3rd instant you commented upon literary pensions and the *status* of literary men in this country, and illustrated your argument by extracts from the story of 'Pendennis,' at present in course of publication. You have received my writings with so much kindness that, if you have occasion to disapprove of them or the author, I can't question your right to blame me, or doubt for a moment the friendliness and honesty of my critic; and however I might dispute the justice of your verdict in my case, I had proposed to submit to it in silence, being indeed very quiet in my conscience with regard to the charge made against me. But another newspaper of high character and repute takes occasion to question the principles advocated in your article of Thursday; arguing in favour of pensions for literary persons, as you argued against them; and the only point upon which the *Examiner* and the *Chronicle* appear to agree unluckily regards myself, who am offered up to general reprehension in two leading articles by the two writers: by the latter, for 'fostering a baneful prejudice' against literary men; by the former, for 'stooping to flatter' this prejudice in the public mind, and condescending to caricature (as is too often my habit) my literary fellow-labourers, in order to pay court to 'the non-literary class.' The charges of the *Examiner* against a man who has never, to his knowledge, been ashamed of his profession, or (except for its dullness) of any single line from his pen—grave as they are, are, I hope, not proven. 'To stoop to flatter' any class is a novel accusation brought against my writings; and as for my scheme, 'to pay court to the non-literary class by disparaging my literary fellow-labourers,' it is a design which would exhibit a degree not only of baseness but of folly upon my part, of which, I trust, I am not capable. The editor of the *Examiner* may, perhaps, occasionally write, like other authors, in a hurry, and not be aware of the conclusions to which some of his sentences may lead. If I stoop to flatter anybody's prejudice for some interested motives of my own, I am no more nor less than a rogue and a cheat: which deductions from the *Examiner's* premises I will not stoop to contradict, because the premises themselves are simply absurd. I deny that the considerable body of our countrymen described by the *Examiner* as 'the non-literary class' has the least gratification in witnessing the degradation or disparagement of literary men. Why accuse 'the non-literary class' of being so ungrateful? If the writings of an author give a reader pleasure or profit, surely the latter will have a favourable opinion of the person who so benefits him. What intelligent man, of what political views, would not receive with respect and welcome that writer of the *Examiner* of whom your paper once said, that 'he made all England laugh and think?' Who would deny to the brilliant wit, that polished satirist, his just tribute of respect and admiration? Does any man who has written a book worth reading—any poet, historian, novelist, man of science—lose reputation by his character for genius or for learning? Does he not, on the contrary, get friends, sympathy, applause—money, perhaps?—all good and pleasant things in themselves, and not ungenerously awarded as they are honestly won. That generous faith in men of letters, that kindly regard in which the whole reading nation holds them, appear to me to be so clearly shown in our country every day, that to question them would be as absurd as, permit me to say for my part, it would be ungrateful. What is it that fills mechanics' institutes in the great provincial towns when literary men are invited to attend their festivals? Has not every literary man of mark his friends and his circle, his hundreds or his tens of thousands of readers? And has not every one had from these constant and affecting testimonials of the esteem in which they hold him? It is of course one writer's lot, from the nature of his subject or of his genius, to command the sympathies or awaken the curiosity of many more readers than shall choose to listen to another author; but surely all get their hearing. The literary profession is not held in disrepute; nobody wants to disparage it; no man loses his social rank, whatever it may be, by practising it. On the contrary, the pen gives a place in the world to men who had none before—a fair place fairly achieved by their genius; as any other degree of eminence is by any other kind of merit. Literary men need not, as it seems to me, be in the least querulous about their position any more, or want the pity of anybody. The money-prizes which the chief among them get are not so high as those which fall to men of other callings—to bishops, or to judges, or to opera-singers and actors; nor have they received stars and garters as yet, or peerages and governorships of islands, such as fall to the lot of military officers. The rewards of the profession are not to be measured by the money-standard: for one man spends a life of learning and labour on a book which does not pay the printer's bill, and another gets a little fortune by a few light volumes. But, putting the money out of the question, I believe that the social estimation of the man of letters is as good as it deserves to be, and as good as that of any other professional man. With respect to the question in debate between you and the *Examiner* as to the propriety of public rewards and honours for literary men, I don't see why men of letters should not very cheerfully coincide with Mr. *Examiner* in accepting all the honours, places, and prizes which they can get. The amount of such as will be awarded to them will not, we may be pretty sure, impoverish the country much; and if it is the custom of the State to reward by money, or titles of honour, or stars and garters of any sort, individuals who do the country service, and if individuals are gratified at having 'Sir' or 'My lord' appended to their names, or stars and ribands hooked on their coats and waistcoats, as men most undoubtedly are, and as their wives, families, and relations are, there can be no reason why men of letters should not have the chance, as well as men of the robe or the sword; or why, if honour and money are good for one profession, they should not be good for another. No man in other callings thinks himself degraded by receiving a reward from his Government; nor, surely, need the literary man be more squeamish about pensions, and ribands, and titles, than the ambassador, or general, or judge. Every European State but ours rewards its men of letters; the American Government gives them their full share of its small patronage; and if Americans, why not Englishmen? If Pitt Crawley is disappointed at not getting a riband on retiring from his diplomatic post at Pumpernickel, if General O'Dowd is pleased to be called Sir Hector O'Dowd, K.C.B., and his wife at being denominated my Lady O'Dowd, are literary men to be the only persons exempt from vanity, and is it to be a sin in them to covet honour? And now, with regard to the charge against myself of fostering baneful prejudices against our calling—to which I no more plead guilty than I should think Fielding would have done if he had been accused of a design to bring the Church into contempt by describing Parson Trulliber—permit me to say, that before you deliver sentence it would be as well if you had waited to hear the whole of the argument. Who knows what is coming in the future numbers of the work which has incurred your displeasure and the *Examiner's*, and whether you, in accusing me of prejudice, and the *Examiner*, (alas!) of swindling

and flattering the public, have not been premature?
Time and the hour may solve this mystery, for
which the candid reader is referred 'to our next.'
That I have a prejudice against running into debt,
and drunkenness, and disorderly life, and against
quackery and falsehood in my profession, I own;
and that I like to have a laugh at those pretenders
in it who write confidential news about fashion
and politics for provincial *gobemouches;* but I am
not aware of feeling any malice in describing this
weakness, or of doing anything wrong in exposing
the former vices. Have they never existed amongst
literary men? Have their talents never been urged
as a plea for improvidence, and their very faults
adduced as a consequence of their genius? The
only moral that I, as a writer, wished to hint in
the descriptions against which you protest, was,
that it was the duty of a literary man, as well as
any other, to practise regularity and sobriety, to
love his family, and to pay his tradesman. Nor
is the picture I have drawn 'a caricature which
I condescend to,' any more than it is a wilful and
insidious design on my part to flatter 'the non-
literary class.' If it be a caricature, it is the

result of a natural perversity of vision, not of an artful desire to mislead: but my attempt was to tell the truth, and I meant to tell it not unkindly. I have seen the bookseller whom Bludyer robbed of his books: I have carried money, and from a noble brother man-of-letters, to some one not unlike Shandon in prison, and have watched the beautiful devotion of his wife in that dreary place. Why are these things not to be described, if they illustrate, as they appear to me to do, that strange and awful struggle of good and wrong which takes place in our hearts and in the world? It may be that I worked out my moral ill, or it may be possible that the critic of the *Examiner* fails in apprehension. My efforts as an artist come perfectly within his province as a censor; but when Mr. *Examiner* says of a gentleman that he is 'stooping to flatter a public prejudice,' which public prejudice does not exist, I submit that he makes a charge which is as absurd as it is unjust; and am thankful that it repels itself. And, instead of accusing the public of persecuting and disparaging us as a class, it seems to me that men of letters had best silently assume that they are as good as any other gentlemen, nor raise piteous controversies upon a question which all people of sense must take to be settled. If I sit at your table, I suppose that I am my neighbour's equal as that he is mine. If I begin straightway with a protest of 'Sir, I am a literary man, but I would have you to know I am as good as you,' which of us is it that questions the dignity of the literary profession—my neighbour who would like to eat his soup in quiet, or the man of letters who commences the argument? And I hope that a comic writer, because he describes one author as improvident, and another as a parasite, may not only be guiltless of a desire to vilify his profession, but may really have its honour at heart. If there are no spendthrifts or parasites amongst us, the satire becomes unjust; but if such exist, or have existed, they are as good subjects for comedy as men of other callings. I never heard that the Bar felt itself aggrieved because 'Punch' chose to describe Mr. Dunup's notorious state of insolvency, or that the picture of Stiggins in 'Pickwick' was intended as an insult to all Dissenters, or that all the attorneys in the empire were indignant at the famous history of the firm of 'Quirk, Gammon, and Snap;' are we to be passed over because we are faultless, or because we cannot afford to be laughed at? And if every character in a story is to represent a class, not an individual—if every bad figure is to have its obliged contrast of a good one, and a balance of vice and virtue is to be struck—novels, I think, would become impossible, as they would be intolerably stupid and unnatural, and there would be a lamentable end of writers and readers of such compositions.

"Believe me, Sir, to be your very faithful Servant,

"W. M. THACKERAY."

It was a peculiarity of Mr. Thackeray to feel annoyed at adverse criticism, and to show his annoyance in a way which more cautious men generally abstain from. He did not conceal his feeling when an unjust attack was levelled at him in an influential journal. He was not one of those remonstrators who never see anything in the papers, but have their "attention called" to them by friends. If he had seen, he frankly avowed that he had seen the attack, and did not scruple to reply if he had an opportunity, and the influence of the journal or reviewer made it worth while, and with the *Times* he had very early had a bout of this kind. When the little account of the funeral of Napoleon in 1840 was published, the *Times*, as he said, rated him, and talked in "its own great roaring way about the flippancy and conceit of Titmarsh," to which he had replied by a sharp paragraph or two. In 1850 a more elaborate attack in the chief journal roused his satirical humour more completely. The article which contained the offence was on the subject of his Christmas Book, entitled "The Knickleburys on the Rhine," published in Dec. 1850, upon which a criticism appeared in that journal, beginning with the following passage:—

"It has been customary, of late years, for the purveyors of amusing literature—the popular authors of the day—to put forth certain opuscules, denominated 'Christmas Books,' with the ostensible intention of swelling the tide of exhilaration, or other expansive emotions, incident upon the exodus of the old and the inauguration of the new year. We have said that their ostensible intention was such, because there is another motive for these productions, locked up (as the popular author deems) in his own breast, but which betrays itself, in the quality of the work, as his principal incentive. Oh! that any muse should be set upon a high stool to cast up accounts and balance a ledger! Yet so it is; and the popular author finds it convenient to fill up the declared deficit and place himself in a position the more effectually to encounter those liabilities which sternly assert themselves contemporaneously and in contrast with the careless and free-handed tendencies of the season by the emission of Christmas books—a kind of literary *assignats*, representing to the emitter expunged debts, to the receiver an investment of enigmatical value. For the most part bearing the stamp of their origin in the vacuity of the writer's exchequer rather than in the fullness of his genius, they suggest by their feeble flavour the rinsings of a void brain after the more important concoctions of the expired year. Indeed, we should as little think of taking these compositions as examples of the merits of their authors as we should think of measuring the valuable services of Mr. Walker, the postman, or Mr. Bell, the dust-collector, by the copy of verses they leave at our doors as a provocative of the expected annual gratuity—effusions with which they may fairly be classed for their intrinsic worth no less than their ultimate purport."

Upon this, and upon some little peculiarities of style in the review, such as a passage in which the learned critic compared the author's satirical attempts to the sardonic divings after the pearl of truth, whose lustre is eclipsed in the display of the diseased oyster, Mr. Thackeray replied in the preface to a second edition of the little book, published a few days later, and entitled "An Essay on Thunder and Small Beer." The style of the *Times* critique, which was generally attributed to the late Mr. Samuel Phillips, afforded too tempting a subject for the satirical pen of the author of "Vanity Fair" to be passed over. The easy humour with which he exposed the pompous affectation of superiority in his critic, the tawdry style and droll logic of his censor, whom he likened not to the awful thunderer of Printing House-square, but to the thunderer's man " Jupiter Jeames, trying to dazzle and roar like his awful employer," afforded the town, through the newspapers which copied the essay, an amount of amusement not often derived from an author's defence of himself from adverse criticism. The essay was remembered long after, when work after work of Mr. Thackeray was severely handled in the same paper, and the recollection of it gave a shadow of support to the theory by which some persons, on the recent occasion of Mr. Thackeray's death, endeavoured to explain the fact that the obituary notice in the *Times*, and the account of his funeral, were more curt than those of any other journal, while the *Times* alone, of all the daily papers, omitted to insert a leading article on the subject of the great loss which had been sustained by the world of letters.

In 1851, Mr. Thackeray appeared in an entirely new character, but one which subsequently proved so lucrative to him, that to this cause, even more than the labours of his pen, must be attributed that easy fortune which he had accumulated before he died. In May of that year he commenced a series of lectures on the English Humourists. The subjects were, Swift; Congreve and Addison; Steele; Prior, Gay, and Pope; Hogarth, Smollet and Fielding, and Sterne and Goldsmith. The lectures were delivered at Willis's Rooms. The price of admission was high, and his audience was numerous, and of the most select kind. It was not composed of that sort of people who crowd to pick up information in the shape of facts with which they have been previously unacquainted, but those who, knowing the eminence of the lecturer, wished to hear his opinion on a subject of national interest. One of the two great humourists of the present age was about to utter his sentiments on the humourists of the age now terminated, and the occasion was sufficient to create an interest which not even the attractive power of the Great Exhibition, then open, could check. The newspapers complained slightly of the low key in which the lecturer spoke, from which cause many of his best points were sometimes lost to the more distant of his auditors.

"In other respects," says the *Times*, "we cannot too highly praise the style of his delivery." Abstaining from rant and gesticulation, he relied for his effect too on the matter which he uttered, and it was singular to see how the isolated pictures, which by a few magic touches descended into the hearts of his hearers. Among the most conspicuous of the literary ladies at this gathering was Miss Brontë, the authoress of "Jane Eyre." She had never before seen the author of "Vanity Fair," though the second edition of her own celebrated novel was dedicated to him by her, with the assurance that she regarded him "as the social regenerator of his day—as the very master of that working corps who would restore to rectitude the warped state of things." Mrs. Gaskell tells us that, when the lecture was over, the lecturer descended from the platform, and making his way towards her, frankly asked her for her opinion. "This," adds Miss Brontë's biographer, "she mentioned to me not many days afterwards, adding remarks almost identical with those which I subsequently read in 'Villette,' where a similar action on the part of M. Paul

Emanuel is related." The remarks of this singular woman upon Mr. Thackeray and his writings, and her accounts of her interviews with him, are curious: they will be found scattered about Mrs. Gaskell's popular biography. Readers of the "Cornhill Magazine" will not have forgotten Mr. Thackeray's affectionate and discriminating sketch of her, which appears some years later in that periodical.

The course was perfectly successful, and the Lectures, subsequently reprinted, rank among the most beautiful writings. They were delivered again soon afterwards in some of the provincial cities, including Edinburgh. A droll anecdote was related at this period in the newspapers, in connection with these provincial appearances.

Previously to delivering them in Scotland, the lecturer bethought himself of addressing them to the rising youth of our two great nurseries of the national mind; and it was necessary, before appearing at Oxford, to obtain the license of the authorities—a very laudable arrangement of course. The Duke of Wellington was the Chancellor, who, if applied to would doubtless have understood at once the man and his business. The Duke lives in the broad atmosphere of the every-day world, and a copy of the "Snob Papers" is on a snug shelf at Walmer Castle. But his dignity at Oxford, on whom the modest applicant waited, knew less about such trifles as "Vanity Fair" and "Pendennis." "Pray what can I do to serve you, sir?" inquired the bland functionary. "My name is Thackeray." "So I see by this card." "I seek permission to lecture within the precincts." "Ah! you are a lecturer; what subjects do you undertake—religious or political?" "Neither; I am a literary man." "Have you written anything?" "Yes; I am the author of 'Vanity Fair.'" "I presume a dissenter—has that anything to do with John Bunyan's book?" "Not exactly; I have also written 'Pendennis.'" "Never heard of these works; but no doubt they are proper books." "I have also contributed to 'Punch.'" "'Punch!' I have heard of that; is it not a ribald publication?"

An invitation to deliver the lectures in America speedily followed. The public interest which heralded his coming in the United States was such as could hardly have been expected for a writer of fiction, who had won his fame by so little appeal to the love of exciting scenes.

His visit (as an American critic remarked,) at least demonstrated, that if they were unwilling to pay English authors for their books, they were ready to reward them handsomely for the opportunity of seeing and hearing them.

At first, the public feeling on the other side of the Atlantic had been very much divided as to his probable reception. "He'll come and humbug us, eat our dinners, pocket our money, and go home and abuse us, like Dickens," said Jonathan, chafing with the remembrance of that grand ball at the Park Theatre, and the Boz tableaux, and the universal wining and dining, to which the author of "Pickwick" was subject while he was our guest. "Let him have his say," said others, "and we will have our look. We will pay a dollar to hear him, if we can see him at the same time; and as for the abuse, why it takes even more than two such cubs of the roaring British lion to frighten the American eagle. Let him come, and give him fair play." He did come, and certainly had his fair play. There was certainly no disappointment with his lectures. Those who knew his books found the author in the lecturer. Those who did not know the books, says one critic, " were charmed in the lecturer by what is charming in the author, the unaffected humanity, the tenderness, the sweetness, the genial play of fancy, and the sad touch of truth, with that glancing stroke of satire, which, lightning-like, illumines while it withers." He did not visit the West, nor Canada. He went home without seeing Niagara Falls. But wherever he did go, he found a generous social welcome, and a respectful and sympathetic hearing. He came to fulfil no mission; but it was felt that his visit had knit more closely the sympathy of the Americans with Englishmen. Heralded by various romantic memoirs, he smiled at them, stoutly asserted that he had been always able to command a good dinner, and to pay for it; nor did he seek to disguise that he hoped his American tour would help him to command and pay for more. He promised not to write a book about the Americans, and he kept his word.

His first lecture was delivered to a crowded audience. On the 19th of November, he commenced his lectures before the Mercantile Library Association, in the spacious New York Church belonging to the congregation presided over by the Rev. Dr. Chapin.

Before many days, the publishers told the world that the subject of Mr. Thackeray's talk had given start to a Swift and Congreve and Addison furor. The booksellers were driving a thrifty trade in forgotten volumes of "Old English Essayists;" the "Spectator" found its way again to the parlour-tables; old "Sir Roger de Coverley" was waked up from his long sleep. "Tristram Shandy" even, was almost forgiven his lewdness; and the "Ass of Melun," and poor Le Fevre were studied wistfully, and placed on the library-table between "Gulliver" and the "Rake's Progress." Girls were working Maria's pet lamb upon their samplers; and hundreds of Lilliput literary ladies were twitching the mammoth Gulliver's whiskers.

The newspaper gossippers were no less busy in noting every personal characteristic of the author.

One remarks :—" As for the man himself who has inoculated us, he is a stout, healthful, broad-shouldered specimen of a man, with cropped greyish hair, and keenish grey eyes, peering very sharply through a pair of spectacles that have a very satirical focus. He seems to stand strongly on his own feet, as if he would not be easily blown about or upset, either by praise or pugilists; a man of good digestion, who takes the world easy, and scents all shams and humours (straightening them between his thumb and forefinger) as he would a pinch of snuff." A London letter of the time says :—" The New York Journalists preserve, on the whole, a delicate silence (very creditable to them) on the subject of Mr. Thackeray's nose; but they are eloquent about his legs; and when the last mail left, a controversy was raging among them on this matter, one party maintaining that 'he stands very firm on his legs,' while the opposition asserted that his legs were decidedly 'shaky.' "

These, however, were light matters compared with the notices in other newspapers which unscrupulously raked together, for the amusement of their readers, details which were mostly untrue, and where true, were of too private a character for public discussion. This led to a humorous remonstrance, forwarded by Mr. Thackeray to " Fraser's Magazine," where it appeared with the signature of " John Small." In this he gave a droll parody of his newspaper biographers' style, which caused some resentment on the part of the writers attacked. One transatlantic defender of the New York press said that " the two most personal accounts of Thackeray published appeared in some Liverpool paper, and in the London *Spectator ;* " adding, " the London correspondents of some of the provincial papers spare nothing of fact or comment touching the private life of public characters. Nay, are there not journals expressly devoted to the contemporary biography of titled, wealthy, and consequential personages, which will tell you how, and in what company, they eat, drink, and travel; their itinerary from the country to London, and from the metropolis to the Continent; the probable marriages, alliances, &c. ? No journal can be better acquainted with these conditions of English society than the classical and vivacious ' Fraser.' Why, then, does John Small address that London editor from New York, converting some paltry and innocent-enough penny-a-liner notice of the author of ' Vanity Fair ' into an enormous national sin and delinquency."

Among the lectures delivered at New York, before he quitted the gay circles of that Empire City for Boston, was one in behalf of a charity ; and the charity lecture was stated to be a melange of all the others, closing very appropriately with an animated tribute to the various, literary, social, and humane qualities of Mr. Charles Dickens. "Papa," he describes his daughter as exclaiming, "Papa, I like Mr. Dickens's book much better than yours."

The remonstrance of John Small in "Fraser," however, did not conclude without a warm acknowledgment of the general kindness he had received in America, so beautifully expressed in his last lecture of the series, delivered on the 7th of April. "In England," he said, " it was my custom, after the delivery of these lectures, to point such a moral as seemed to befit the country I lived in, and to protest against an outcry which some brother authors of mine most imprudently and unjustly raise, when they say that our profession is neglected and its professors held in light esteem. Speaking in this country, I would say that such a complaint could not only not be advanced, but could not even be understood here, where your men of letters take their manly share in public life; whence Everett goes as minister to Washington, and Irving and Bancroft to represent the republic in the old country. And if to English authors the English public is, as I believe, kind and just in the main, can any of us say, will any who visit your country not proudly and gratefully own, with what a cordial and generous greeting you receive us? I look around on this great company. I think of my gallant young patrons of the Mercantile Library Association, as whose servant I appear before you, and of the kind hand stretched out to welcome me by men famous in letters, and honoured in our own country as in their own, and I thank you and them for a most kindly greeting and a most generous hospitality. At home and amongst his own people, it scarce becomes an English writer to speak of himself;

his public estimation must depend on his works; his private esteem on his character and his life. But here, among friends newly found, I ask leave to say that I am thankful; and I think with a grateful heart of those I leave behind me at home, who will be proud of the welcome you hold out to me, and will benefit, please God, when my days of work are over, by the kindness which you show to their father."

A still more interesting paper was his Preface to Messrs. Appleton and Co.'s New York edition of his minor works. Readers will remember Mr. Thackeray's droll account, in one of his lectures, of his first interview with the agent of Appleton and Co., when holding on, sea-sick, to the bulwarks of the New York steam-vessel on his outward voyage. The preface referred to contains evidence that the appeal of the energetic representative of that well-known publishing house was not altogether fruitless. It is as follows:—

"On coming into this country I found that the projectors of this series of little books had preceded my arrival by publishing a number of early works, which have appeared under various pseudonyms during the last fifteen years. I was not the master to choose what stories of mine should appear or not; these miscellanies were all advertised, or in course of publication; nor have I had the good fortune to be able to draw a pen, or alter a blunder of author or printer, except in the case of the accompanying volumes which contain contributions to 'Punch,' whence I have been enabled to make something like a selection. In the 'Letters of Mr. Brown,' and the succeeding short essays and descriptive pieces, something graver and less burlesque was attempted than in other pieces which I here publish. My friend, the 'Fat Contributor,' accompanied Mr. Titmarsh in his 'Journey from Cornhill to Cairo.' The prize novels contain imitations of the writings of some contemporaries who still live and flourish in the novelists' calling. I myself had scarcely entered on it when these burlesque tales were begun, and stopped further parody from a sense that this merry task of making fun of the novelists should be left to younger hands than my own; and, in a little book published some four years since, in England, by my friends Messrs. Hannay and Shirley Brooks, I saw a caricature of myself and writings to the full, as ludicrous and faithful as the prize novels of Mr. Punch. Nor was there, had I desired it, any possibility of preventing the reappearance of these performances. Other publishers, besides the Messrs. Appleton, were ready to bring my hidden works to the light. Very many of the other books printed, I have not seen since their appearance twelve years ago, and it was with no small feelings of curiosity (remembering under what sad circumstances the tale had been left unfinished) that I bought the incomplete 'Shabby Genteel Story,' in a railway car, on my first journey from Boston hither, from a rosy-cheeked, little peripatetic book merchant, who called out 'Thackeray's Works,' in such a kind, gay voice, as gave me a feeling of friendship and welcome.

"There is an opportunity of being either satiric or sentimental. The careless papers written at an early period, and never seen since the printer's boy carried them away, are brought back and laid at the father's door; and he cannot, if he would, forget or disown his own children.

"Why were some of the little brats brought out of their obscurity? I own to a feeling of anything but pleasure in reviewing some of these misshapen juvenile creatures, which the publisher has disinterred and resuscitated. There are two performances especially, (among the critical and biographical works of the erudite Mr. Yellowplush) which I am very sorry to see reproduced; and I ask pardon of the author of the 'Caxtons' for a lampoon, which I know he himself has forgiven, and which I wish I could recall.

"I had never seen that eminent writer but once in public when this satire was penned, and wonder at the recklessness of the young man who could fancy such personality was harmless jocularity, and never calculate that it might give pain. The best experiences of my life have been gained since that time of youth and gaiety, and careless laughter. I allude to them, perhaps, because I would not have any kind and friendly American reader judge of me by the wild performances of early years. Such a retrospect as the sight of these old acquaintances perforce occasioned, cannot, if it would, be gay. The old scenes return, the remembrance of the bygone time, the chamber in which the stories were written, the faces that shone round the table.

"Some biographers in this country have been pleased to depict that homely apartment after a very strange and romantic fashion; and an author in the direst struggles of poverty, waited upon by a family domestic in 'all the splendour of his menial decorations,' has been circumstantially described to the reader's amusement as well as to the writer's own. I may be permitted to assure the former that the splendour and the want were alike fanciful; and that the meals were not only sufficient but honestly paid for.

"That extreme liberality with which American publishers have printed the works of English authors has had at least this beneficial result for us, that our names and writings are known by multitudes using our common mother tongue, who never had heard of us or our books but for the speculators who have sent them all over this continent.

"It is, of course, not unnatural for the English writer to hope that some day he may share a portion of the profits which his works bring at present to the persons who vend them in this country; and I am bound gratefully to say myself, that since my arrival here I have met with several publishing houses who are willing to acknowledge our little claim to participate in the advantages arising out of our books; and the present writer having long since ascertained that a portion of a loaf is more satisfactory than no bread at all, gratefully accepts and acknowledges several slices which the book-purveyors in this city have proffered to him of their own free-will.

"If we are not paid in full and in specie as yet, English writers surely ought to be thankful for the very great kindness and friendliness with which the American public receives them; and if in hope some day that measures may pass here to legalize our right to profit a little by the commodities which we invent and in which we deal, I for one can cheerfully say that the good-will towards us from publishers and public is undoubted, and wait for still better times with perfect confidence and humour.

"If I have to complain of any special hardship, it is, not that our favourite works are reproduced, and our children introduced to the American public—children whom we have educated with care, and in whom we take a little paternal pride—but that ancient magazines are ransacked, and shabby old articles dragged out, which we had gladly left in the wardrobes where they have lain hidden many years. There is no control, however, over a man's thoughts—once uttered and printed, back they may come upon us on any sudden day; and in this collection which Messrs. Appleton are publishing, I find two or three such early productions of my own that I gladly would take back, but that they have long since gone out of the paternal guardianship.

"If not printed in this series, they would have appeared from other presses, having not the slightest need of the author's own imprimatur; and I cannot sufficiently condole with a literary gentleman of this city, who (in his voyages of professional adventure) came upon an early performance of mine, which shall be nameless, carried the news of the discovery to a publisher of books, and had actually done me the favour to sell my book to that liberal man; when, behold, Messrs. Appleton announced the book in the press, and my *confrère* had to refund the prize-money which had been paid to him. And if he is a little chagrined at finding other intrepid voyagers beforehand with him in taking possession of my island, and the American flag already floating there, he will understand the feelings of the harmless but kindly-treated aboriginal who makes every sign of peace, who smokes the pipe of submission, and meekly acquiesces in his own annexation.

. "It is said that those only who win should laugh: I think, in this case, my readers will not grudge the losing side its share of harmless good-humour. If I have contributed to theirs, or provided them with means of amusement, I am glad to think my books have found favour with the American public, as I am proud to own the great and cordial welcome with which they have received me.

"W. M. THACKERAY.

"New York, December, 1852."

Such words could not fail to be gratifying to the American people, as an evidence of Thackeray's sense of the reception he had received, and in spite of a slight misunderstanding founded on a mistake and speedily cleared up, it may be said that no English writer of fiction was ever more popular in the United States.

The publication of "The Adventures of Henry Esmond," which appeared just as its author was starting for America in 1852, marked an important epoch in his career. It was a continuous story, and one worked out with closer attention to the thread of the narrative than he had hitherto produced—a fact due, no doubt, partly to its appearance in three volumes complete, instead of in detached monthly portions. But its most striking feature was its elaborate imitation of the style and even the manner of thought of the time of Queen Anne's reign, in which its scenes were laid. The preparation of his Lectures on the Humourists had, no doubt, suggested to him the idea of writing a story of this kind, as it afterwards suggested to him the design of writing a history of that period which he had long entertained, but in which he had, we believe, made no progress when he died. But his fondness for the Queen Anne writers was of older date. Affectionate allusions to Sir Richard Steele—like himself a Charterhouse boy—and to Addison, and Pope, and Swift, may be found in his earliest magazine articles. That the style with which the author of " Vanity Fair " and " Pendennis " had so often delighted his readers was to some degree formed upon those models so little studied in his boyhood, cannot be doubted by any one who is familiar with the literature of the Augustan age. The writers of that period were fond of French models, as the writers of Elizabeth's time looked to Italy for their literary inspiration; but there was no time when English prose was generally written with more purity and ease; for the translation of the Scriptures, which is generally referred to as an evidence of the perfection of our English speech in Elizabeth's time, owed its strength and simplicity chiefly to the rejection by the pious translators of the scholarly style most in vogue, in favour of the homely English then current among the people. If we except the pamphlet writers of earlier reigns, the Queen Anne writers were the first who systematically wrote for the people in plain Saxon English, not easy to imitate in these days. "Esmond" was from the first most liked among literary men who can appreciate a style having no resemblance to the fashion of the day; but there was a vein of tenderness and true pathos in the story which, in spite of some objectionable features in the plot, and of a somewhat wearisome genealogical introduction, have by degrees gained for it a high rank among the author's works. "Esmond" was followed by "The Newcomes," in 1855, a work which revealed a deeper pathos than any of his previous novels, and showed that the author could, when he pleased, give us pictures of moral beauty and loveliness. In this work he returned to the yellow numbers in the old monthly form.

An incident in connection with the publication of "The Newcomes" may here be mentioned. Mr. Thackeray's fondness for irony had frequently brought him into disgrace with people not so ready as himself for understanding that dangerous figure. A passage in one of his chapters of this story alluding to "Mr. Washington," in a parody of the style of the *British Patriot*, of the times of the War of Independence, was so far misunderstood in America that the fact was alluded to by the New York correspondent of the *Times*. Upon which Mr. Thackeray addressed the following letter to that journal:—

"Sir,—Allow me a word of explanation in answer to a strange charge which has been brought against me in the United States, and which your New York correspondent has made public in this country.

"In the first number of a periodical story which I am now publishing, appears a sentence in which I should never have thought of finding any harm until it has been discovered by some critics over the water. The fatal words are these:—

"'When pigtails grew on the backs of the British gentry, and their wives wore cushions on their heads, over which they tied their own hair, and disguised it with powder and pomatum; when ministers went in their stars and orders to the House of Commons, and the orators of the opposition attacked nightly the noble lord in the blue riband; when Mr. Washington was heading the American rebels with a courage, it must be confessed, worthy of a better cause,—there came to London, out of a northern county, Mr., etc.'

"This paragraph has been interpreted in America as an insult to Washington and the whole Union; and from the sadness and gravity with which your correspondent quotes certain of my words, it is evident he, too, thinks they have an insolent and malicious meaning.

"Having published the American critic's comment, permit the author of a faulty sentence to say what he did mean, and to add the obvious moral of the apologue which has been so oddly construed. I am speaking of a young apprentice coming to London between the years 1770 and '80, and want to depict a few figures of the last century. (The illustrated head-letter of the chapter was intended to represent Hogarth's 'Industrious Apprentice.') I fancy the old society, with its hoops and powder—Barré or Fox thundering at Lord North asleep on the Treasury bench—the news readers at the coffee-room talking over the paper, and owning that this Mr. Washington who was leading the rebels, was a very courageous soldier, and worthy of a better cause than fighting against King George. The images are at least natural and pretty consecutive. 1776—the people of London in '76—the Lords and House of Commons in '76—Lord North—Washington—what tho people thought about Washington—I am thinking about '76. Where, in the name of common sense, is the insult to 1853? The satire, if satire there be, applies to us at home, who called Washington 'Mr. Washington;' as we called Frederick the Great 'the Protestant Hero,' or Napoleon 'The Corsican Tyrant,' or 'General Bonaparte.' Need I say, that our officers were instructed (until they were taught better manners) to call Washington 'Mr. Washington?' and that the Americans were called rebels during the whole of that contest? Rebels!—of course they were rebels; and I should like to know what native American would not have been a rebel in that cause?

"As irony is dangerous, and has hurt the feelings of kind friends whom I would not wish to offend, let me say, in perfect faith and gravity, that I think the cause for which Washington fought entirely just and right, and the champion the very noblest, purest, bravest, best of God's men.

"I am, Sir, your very faithful servant,
"W. M. THACKERAY.
"Athenæum, Nov. 22."

Another journey to the United States, equally successful, and equally profitable in a pecuniary sense, was the chief event in his life in 1856. The lectures delivered were those beautiful anecdotical and reflective discourses on the "Four Georges," made familiar to readers by their publication in the "Cornhill Magazine," and since then, in a separate form. The subject was not favourable to the display of the author's more genial qualities. Very little that is good could be said of the Georges. Yet, where in English literature could we find anything more solemn and affecting than his picture of the old King, the last of that name? When "all light, all reason, all sound of human voices, all the pleasures of this world of God were taken from him." Concluding with the affecting appeal to his American audience—" O brothers! speaking the same dear mother tongue—O comrades! enemies no more,

let us take a mournful hand together as we stand
by this royal corpse, and call a truce to battle!
Low he lies to whom the proudest used to kneel
once, and who was cast lower than the poorest—
dead whom millions prayed for in vain. Hush,
Strife and Quarrels over the solemn grave!
Sound Trumpets, a mournful march. Fall, Dark
Curtain, upon his pageant, his pride, his grief, his
awful tragedy!"

These lectures were successfully repeated in
England. Mr. Thackeray, indeed, was now recognized as one of the most attractive lecturers of
the day. His appearance, whether in lecturing on
the "Georges" for his own profit, or on "Weekday Preachers," or some other topic for the benefit of the families of deceased brother writers, such
as the late Mr. Angus B. Reach and Mr. Douglas
Jerrold, always attracted the most cultivated
classes of the various cities in which he appeared;
but an attempt to draw together a large audience
of the less educated classes by giving a course of
lectures at the great Music Hall, was less happy.
In Edinburgh, his reception was always in the
highest degree successful. He was more exten-

sively known and admired among the intellectual portion of the people of Scotland than any living writer, not excepting Mr. Thomas Carlyle. There was something in his peculiar genius that commended him to the Northern temperament. About seven years before Thackeray was delivering his lectures on the "Four Georges" in Scotland, to larger and more intellectual audiences than ever listened to any other lecturer, and he lectured there since for the benefit of Mr. Angus B. Reach's widow. Nearly all the men of Edinburgh, with any tincture of literature, had met him personally, and a few knew him well. He was almost the only great author that the majority of the lovers of literature in it had seen and heard, and his form and figure and voice, with its tragic tones and pauses, well entitled him to take his place in any ideal rank of giants. He was much gratified (says Mr. Hannay) by the success of the "Four Georges,"—(a series which superseded an earlier scheme for as many discourses on "Men of the World,")—in Scotland. "I have had three per cent. of the whole population here;" he wrote from Edinburgh in November,

1856,—" If I could but get three per cent. out of London ! "

Most of Mr. Thackeray's readers will remember, that in 1857, he was invited by some friends to offer himself as a candidate for the representation in Parliament of the City of Oxford. Mr. Hannay, in his graceful and affectionate memoir of Thackeray, published in the *Edinburgh Courant*, tells his readers, with a national zeal for his party, that the radicals hated Mr. Thackeray as the associate of aristocratic personages. But the radical party had no ground for such a feeling. From his earliest life he had professed strong liberal views; and he maintained them to the last. An accident brought him into connexion with the scurrilous Tory writers who formed the staff of " Fraser," but his own papers in that magazine had nothing to do with politics; and no hints will be found in them of sympathy with the political views of his associates. In 1836, when writing for the *Constitutional*, he wrote strongly in favour of advanced liberal views. In 1857, when a prosperous man, he contested the vacant borough of Oxford against the Government candidate, as an advocate of the Ballot—a fact which brought down upon him still more strongly the ready pens who write under Government inspiration in the *Times.* But the following papers from his Address to the Electors of Oxford, will best show his views on politics at this time.

"GENTLEMEN,—I should be unworthy of the great kindness and cordiality with which you have received me to-night, were I to hesitate to put your friendship to the test and ask you to confirm it at the poll.

* * * * * *

"I would use my best endeavours not merely to enlarge the constituencies, but to popularize the Government of this country. With no feeling but that of good-will towards those leading aristocratic families, who are administering the chief offices of the State, I believe that it could be benefited by the skill and talents of persons less aristocratic, and that the country thinks so likewise.

"I think that to secure the due freedom of representation, and to defend the poor voter from the chance of intimidation, the ballot is the best safeguard we know of, and would vote most hopefully for that measure. I would have the suffrage amended in nature, as well as in numbers; and hope to see many educated classes represented who have now no voice in elections.

* * * * * *

"The usefulness of a Member of Parliament is best

tested at home; and should you think fit to elect me as your representative, I promise to use my utmost endeavour to increase and advance the social happiness, the knowledge, and the power of the people.

"W. M. THACKERAY.

"Mitre, July 9, 1857."

At the hustings he spoke as follows :—

"As I came down to this place, I saw on each side of me placards announcing that there was no manner of doubt that on Tuesday the friends of the Right Hon. Edward Cardwell would elect him to a seat in Parliament. I also saw other placards announcing in similar terms a confidence that there was no doubt that I should be elected to a seat in Parliament for the City of Oxford. Now as both sides are perfectly confident of success—as I for my part, feel perfectly confident, and as my opponents entertain the same favourable opinion in regard to themselves—surely both sides may meet here in perfect good-humour. I hear that not long since—in the memory of many now alive—this independent city was patronized by a great university, and that a great duke, who lived not very far from here, at the time of election used to put on his boots and ride down and order the freemen of Oxford to elect a member for him. Any man who has wandered through your beautiful city as I have done within these last few days cannot but be struck with the difference between the ancient splendour, the academic grandeur that prevailed in this place—the processions of dons, doctors, and proctors—and your new city, which is not picturesque or beautiful at all, but which contains a number of streets, peopled by thousands of hard-working, honest, rough-handed men. These men have grown up of late years, and have asserted their determination to have a representative of their own. Such a representative they found three months ago, and such a representative they returned to Parliament in the person of my friend, Mr. Neate.* But such a representative was turned out of that Parliament by a sentence which I cannot call unjust, because he himself is too magnanimous and generous to say so, but which I will call iniquitous. He was found guilty of a twopennyworth of bribery which he never committed; and a Parliament which has swallowed so many camels, strained at that little gnat, and my friend, your representative, the very best man you could find to represent you was turned back, and you were left without a man. I cannot hope—I never thought to equal him; I only came forward at a moment when I felt it necessary that some one professing his principles, and possessing your confidence, should be ready to step into the gap which he had made. I know that the place was very eagerly sought for by other folks on the other side, entertaining other opinions. Perhaps you don't know that last week there was a Tory baronet down here, walking about in the shade, as umbrageous almost as that under which my opponent, Mr. Cardwell, has sheltered himself.

* Mr. Neate was then Professor of Political Economy in the University.

Of course you know there came down a ministerial nominee—Lord Monck; but you do not know that Mr. Hayter, who is what is called the Whipper-in for the Ministerial party, came down here also on Saturday week in a dark and mysterious manner, and that some conversation took place, the nature of which I cannot pretend to know anything about, because I have no spies, however people may be lurking at the doors of our committee-room. But the result of all was, that Lord Monck disappeared, and Mr. Hayter vanished into darkness and became a myth; and we were informed that a powerful requisition from the City of Oxford had invited Mr. Cardwell. Mind, Mr. Cardwell has given no note in reply—no mark, no sign. We do not know, even now, whether he accepted that polite invitation; we do not know it even to this day, except that his godfathers have been here and have said so. After the manner in which the electors of Oxford have received me, could I possibly have gone back simply because we are told that Mr. Cardwell had received an invitation, which we did not know whether he had accepted or not? I feel it, therefore, to be my humble duty to stand in the place where I found myself. I do not know that I would have ventured to oppose Mr. Cardwell under other circumstances. I am fully aware of his talents. I know his ability as a statesman, and no man can say that I have, during the whole of my canvass, uttered a word at all unfriendly or disrespectful towards that gentleman. I should have hesitated on any other occasion in opposing him, but I cannot hesitate now, because I know that we have the better cause, and that we mean to make that better cause triumphant.

* * * * * *

I say they have, and that any man who belongs to the Peelite party is not the man who ought to be put forward by any constituency at the eve of a great and momentous English war. As to my own opinions on public questions, you may have heard them pretty freely expressed on many occasions. I only hope if you elect me to Parliament, I shall be able to obviate the little difficulty which has been placarded against me—that I could not speak. I own I cannot speak very well, but I shall learn. I cannot spin out glibe sentences by the yard, as some people can; but if I have got anything in my mind, if I feel strongly on any question, I have I believe got brains enough to express it. When you send a man to the House of Commons, you do not want him to be always talking; he goes there to conduct the business of the country; he has to prepare himself on the question on which he proposes to speak before six hundred and fifty-six members, who would be bored if every man were to deliver his opinion. He must feel and understand what he is going to say, and I have not the least doubt that I shall be able to say what I feel and think, if you will give me the chance of saying it. If any one in the House of Commons talked all he thought upon everything, good God! what a Babel it would be! You would not get on at all. On the first night I came among you, many questions were put to me by a friend, who capped them all by saying, 'Now, Mr. Thackeray, are you for the honour of England?' I said that that was rather a wild and a wide question to put, but to the best of my belief I was for the honour of England, and would work for it to the best of my power. About the ballot we are all agreed. If I was for the ballot before I came down here, I am more for the ballot now. As to triennial Parliaments, if the constituents desire them, I am for them."

A voice here inquired if Mr. Thackeray "would have the ballot to-morrow?" and he continued—

"No, we are too manly, too plucky, too honest, and we will beat them without it; but another day, when we have a better representation, we will have the ballot. If you elect me, I shall not go to the House of Commons hostile to the present Ministry, but determined to keep them to their work, and to prevent them from shrinking from any of the promises they have made. I think them in a war crisis eminently the best men to carry on the councils of the country, and to contend against the Tories and Peelites, who have very nearly paralyzed their arms."

The official declaration showed that the popular novelist was beaten by so narrow a majority in a contest with an opponent backed by the powerful support of the Government, as to afford abundant evidence of the favour of the electors. The result was declared on the 21st July, by the Mayor, at six o'clock, and the yard attached to the Townhall was as fully crowded as it had been on the previous morning. The announcement was received with a mixture of cheers and hisses; but on Mr. Thackeray coming forward to address the meeting, he was welcomed with loud and prolonged cheering. He said—

"Give me leave to speak a few words to you on this occasion, for although the red, white and blue are my friends, I hope to make the green and yellow my friends also. Let me tell you a little story, but a true one. Some years ago, when boxing was more common in this country than it is at the present time, two celebrated champions met to fight a battle on Moulsey Heath. Their names were Gully and Gregson. They fought the most tremendous battle that had been known for many long years, and Gregson got the worst of it. As he was lying on his bed some time afterwards, blinded and his eyes closed up, he asked a friend to give him something to drink. A person in the room handed him some drink and grasped him by the hand. 'Whose hand is this?' asked Gregson. ' 'Tis Jack Gully's,' was the reply. Now Gregson was the man who was beaten and Gully was the conqueror, and he was the first man to shake him by the hand, to show him that he had no animosity against him. This should be the conduct of all loyal Englishmen, to fight a good fight, and to hold no animosity against the opposite side. With this feeling I go away from Oxford. With this feeling I shall have redeemed one of the promises I made you yesterday; the other I cannot by any possibility answer, because, somehow or other, our side has come out a little below the other side. I wish to shake Mr. Cardwell by the hand, and to congratulate him on being the representative of this great city. I say it is a victory you ought to be proud of; it is a battle which you ought to be proud of who have taken part in it; you have done your duty nobly and fought most gallantly. I am a man who was unknown to most of you, who only came before you with the recommendation of my noble and excellent friend Mr. Neate, but I have met with many friends. You have fought the battle gallantly against great influences, against an immense strength which have been brought against you, and in favour of that honoured and respected man Mr. Cardwell."

Some hisses having greeted this remark, Mr. Thackeray exclaimed—

"Stop, don't hiss. When Lord Monck came down here and addressed the electors, he was good enough to say a kind word in favour of me. Now, that being the case, don't let me be outdone in courtesy and generosity, but allow me to say a few words of the respect and cordiality which I entertain for Mr. Cardwell. As for the party battle which divides you, I am, gentlemen, a stranger, for I never heard the name of certain tradesmen of this city till I came among you.

Perhaps I thought my name was better known than it is. You, the electors of Oxford, know whether I have acted honestly towards you; and you on the other side will say whether I ever solicited a vote when I knew that vote was promised to my opponent; or whether I have not always said—'Sir, keep your word; here is my hand on it, let us part good friends.' With my opponents I part so. With others, my friends, I part with feelings still more friendly, not only for the fidelity you have shown towards me, but for your noble attachment to the gallant and tried whom you did know, and who I hope will be your representative at some future time."

In answer to a cry of "Bribery," he continued—

"Don't cry out bribery; if you know of it, prove it; but as I am innocent of bribery myself, I do not choose to fancy that other men are not equally loyal and honest. It matters very little whether I am in the House of Commons or not, to prate a little more; but you have shown a great spirit, a great resolution, and great independence; and I trust at some future day, when you know me better than you do now, you will be able to carry your cause to a more successful issue. Before I came to Oxford, I knew that there was a certain question that would go against me, and which I would not blink to be made a duke or a marquis to-morrow. In March last, when I was at a dinner at Edinburgh, some friend of mine asked me to stand for the representation of their city. My answer was this

—' That I was for having the people amused after they had done their worship on a Sunday.' I knew that I was speaking to a people who, of all others, were the most open to scruples on that point, but I did my duty as an honest man, and stated what my opinion was. I have done my duty honestly to this city, and I believe that this is the reason why I am placed in a minority; but I am contented to bow to that decision. I told you that I was for allowing a man to have harmless pleasures when he had done his worship on Sundays. I expected to have a hiss, but they have taken a more dangerous shape—the shape of slander. Those gentlemen who will take the trouble to read my books—and I should be glad to have as many of you for subscribers as will come forward—will be able to say whether there is anything in them that should not be read by any one's children, or by my own, or by any Christian man. I say, on this ground I will retire, and take my place with my pen and ink at my desk, and leave to Mr. Cardwell a business which I am sure he understands better than I do."

A characteristic anecdote has recently been told in the newspapers relating to the Oxford election by one who was staying with Thackeray at his hotel during his contest with Mr. Cardwell. Whilst looking out a window a crowd passed along the street, hooting and handling rather roughly some of Mr. Cardwell's supporters. Mr.

Thackeray started up in the greatest possible excitement, and using some strong expletive, bolted down stairs, and notwithstanding the efforts of some old electioneers to detain him, who happened to be of .opinion that a trifling correction of the opposite party might be beneficial *pour encourager les autres*, he was not to be deterred, and was next seen towering above the crowd, dealing about him right and left, in defence of his opponent's partisans, and in defiance of his own friends.

The year 1858 was marked by an unfortunate episode the facts of which cannot be omitted from this narrative, because though trifling in their origin, they finally led to a temporary estrangement between Mr. Thackeray and his great brother novelist, Mr. Dickens, with whom he had hitherto had only relations of the most friendly character. On the 12th of June in that year an article had appeared in a periodical called "Town Talk," which professed to give an account of Mr. Thackeray—his appearance, his career, and his success. The article was coarse and offensive in tone; but it was notorious that the periodical was edited by a clever writer of the day, well-known to Mr. Thackeray, as a brother member of a club to which he belonged. As such, the subject of the attack felt himself compelled to take notice of it. In order to understand the anger displayed by the latter at this unprovoked attack, it is necessary to quote the following passage from the article:—

"HIS APPEARANCE.

"Mr. Thackeray is forty-six years old, though from the silvery whiteness of his hair he appears somewhat older. He is very tall, standing upwards of six feet two inches; and as he walks erect, his height makes him conspicuous in every assembly. His face is bloodless, and not particularly expressive, but remarkable for the fracture of the bridge of the nose, the result of an accident in youth. He wears a small grey whisker, but otherwise is clean shaven. No one meeting him could fail to recognize in him a gentleman: his bearing is cold and uninviting, his style of conversation either openly cynical or affectedly good-natured and benevolent; his *bonhommie* is forced, his wit biting, his pride easily touched—but his appearance is invariably that of the cool, *suave*, well-bred gentleman, who, whatever may be rankling within, suffers no surface display of his emotion.

"HIS SUCCESS,

"Commencing with 'Vanity Fair,' culminated with his 'Lectures on the English Humourists of the

Eighteenth Century,' which were attended by all the court and fashion of London. The prices were extravagant, the Lecturer's adulation of birth and position was extravagant, the success was extravagant. No one succeeds better than Mr. Thackeray in cutting his coat according to his cloth: here he flattered the aristocracy, but when he crossed the Atlantic, George Washington became the idol of his worship, the 'Four Georges' the objects of his bitterest attacks. These last-named Lectures have been dead failures in England, though as literary compositions they are most excellent. Our own opinion is, that his success is on the wane; his writings never were understood or appreciated even by the middle classes; the aristocracy have been alienated by his American onslaught on their body, and the educated and refined are not sufficiently numerous to constitute an audience; moreover, there is a want of heart in all he writes, which is not to be balanced by the most brilliant sarcasm and the most perfect knowledge of the workings of the human heart."

Two days later Mr. Thackeray addressed the assumed writer of this article, in the following letter:

"36 Onslow-square, S. W., June 14.

"SIR,—I have received two numbers of a little paper called 'Town Talk,' containing notices respecting myself, of which, as I learn from the best authority, you are the writer.

"In the first article of 'Literary Talk' you think fit

to publish an incorrect account of my private dealings with my publishers.

"In this week's number appears a so-called 'Sketch,' containing a description of my manners, person, and conversation, and an account of my literary works, which of course you are at liberty to praise or condemn as a literary critic.

"But you state, with regard to my conversation, that it is either 'frankly cynical or affectedly benevolent and good-natured;' and of my works (Lectures), that in some I showed 'an extravagant adulation of rank and position,' which in other lectures ('as I know how to cut my coat according to my cloth') became the object of my bitterest attack.

"As I understand your phrases, you impute insincerity to me when I speak good-naturedly in private; assign dishonorable motives to me for sentiments which I have delivered in public, and charge me with advancing statements which I have never delivered at all.

"Had your remarks been written by a person unknown to me, I should have noticed them no more than other calumnies; but as we have shaken hands more than once, and met hitherto on friendly terms (you may ask one of your employers, Mr. ——, of ——, whether I did not speak of you very lately in the most friendly manner), I am obliged to take notice of articles which I consider to be not offensive and unfriendly merely, but slanderous and untrue.

'We met at a Club, where, before you were born, I believe, I and other gentlemen have been in the habit

of talking without any idea that our conversation would supply paragraphs for professional vendors of 'Literary Talk;' and I don't remember that out of that Club I have ever exchanged six words with you. Allow me to inform you that the talk which you have heard there is not intended for newspaper remarks; and to beg— as I have a right to do—that you will refrain from printing comments upon my private conversations; that you will forego discussions, however blundering, upon my private affairs; and that you will henceforth please to consider any question of my personal truth and sincerity as quite out of the province of your criticism. I am, &c.
"W. M. THACKERAY."

Subsequently Mr. Thackeray " rather (he said) than have any further correspondence with the writer of the character," determined to submit the letters which had passed between them to the Committee of the Club, for that body to decide whether the practice of publishing such articles would not be " fatal to the comfort of the Club," and " intolerable in a society of gentlemen." The Committee accordingly met, and decided that the writer of the attack complained of was bound to make an ample apology, or to retire from the Club. The latter contested the right of the Committee to interfere. Suits at law and proceedings in Chancery against the committee, were threatened; when Mr. Dickens, who was also a member of the Club, interfered with the following letter:—

"Tavistock House, Tavistock-square, London, W. C.
"Wednesday, 24th November, 1858.

"MY DEAR THACKERAY,—Without a word of prelude, I wish this note to revert to a subject on which I said six words to you at the Athenæum when I last saw you.

"Coming home from my country work, I find Mr. Edwin James's opinion taken on this painful question of the Garrick and Mr. Edmund Yates. I find it strong on the illegality of the Garrick proceeding. Not to complicate this note or give it a formal appearance, I forbear from copying the opinion; but I have asked to see it, and I have it, and I want to make no secret from you of a word of it.

"I find Mr. Edwin James retained on the one side; I hear and read of the Attorney-General being retained on the other. Let me, in this state of things, ask you a plain question.

"Can any conference be held between me, as representing Mr. Yates, and an appointed friend of yours, as representing you, with the hope and purpose of some quiet accommodation of this deplorable matter, which will satisfy the feelings of all concerned?

"It is right that, in putting this to you, I should tell you that Mr. Yates, when you first wrote to him, brought your letter to me. He had recently done me a manly service I can never forget, in some private distress of mine (generally within your knowledge), and he naturally thought of me as his friend in an emergency. I told him that his article was not to be defended; but I confirmed him in his opinion that it was not reasonably possible for him set to right what was amiss, on the receipt of a letter couched in the very strong terms you had employed. When you appealed to the Garrick Committee, and they called their General Meeting, I said at that meeting that you and I had been on good terms for many years, and that I was very sorry to find myself opposed to you; but that I was clear that the Committee had nothing on earth to do with it, and that in the strength of my conviction I should go against them.

"If this mediation that I have suggested can take place, I shall be heartily glad to do my best in it—and God knows in no hostile spirit towards any one, least of all to you. If it cannot take place, the thing is at least no worse than it was; and you will burn this letter, and I will burn your answer.

"Yours faithfully,
"CHARLES DICKENS.
"W. M. Thackeray, Esq."

To this Mr. Thackeray replied:—

"36, Onslow-square, 26th November, 1858.

"DEAR DICKENS,—I grieve to gather from your letter that you were Mr. Yates's adviser in the dispute between me and him. His letter was the cause of my appeal to the Garrick Club for protection from insults against which I had no other remedy.

"I placed my grievance before the Committee of the Club as the only place where I have been accustomed to meet Mr. Yates. They gave their opinion of his conduct and of the reparation which lay in his power. Not satisfied with their sentence, Mr. Yates called for a General Meeting; and, the meeting which he had called having declared against him, he declines the jurisdiction which he had asked for, and says he will have recourse to lawyers.

"You say that Mr. Edwin James is strongly of opinion that the conduct of the Club is illegal. On this point I can give no sort of judgment: nor can I conceive that the Club will be frightened, by the opinion of any lawyer, out of their own sense of the justice and honour which ought to obtain among gentlemen.

"Ever since I submitted my case to the Club, I have had, and can have, no part in the dispute. It is for them to judge if any reconcilement is possible with your friend. I subjoin the copy of a letter which I wrote to the Committee, and refer you to them for the issue.

"Yours, &c.,
"W. M. THACKERAY.

" C. Dickens, Esq."

The enclosure referred to was as follows :—

"Onslow-square, Nov. 28, 1858.

"GENTLEMEN,—I have this day received a communication from Mr. Charles Dickens, relative to the dispute which has been so long pending, in which he says:—

"'Can any conference be held between me as representing Mr. Yates, and any appointed friend of yours, as representing you, in the hope and purpose of some quiet accommodation of this deplorable matter, which will satisfy the feelings of all parties?'

"I have written to Mr. Dickens to say, that since the commencement of this business, I have placed myself entirely in the hands of the Committee of the Garrick, and am still as ever prepared to abide by any decision at which they may arrive on the subject. I conceive I cannot, if I would, make the dispute once more personal, or remove it out of the court to which I submitted it for arbitration.

"If you can devise any peaceful means for ending it, no one will be better pleased than

"Your obliged faithful servant
"W. M. THACKERAY.
"The Committee of the Garrick Club."

It would be in vain to attempt to conceal that this painful affair left a coolness between Mr. Thackeray and his brother novelist. Mr. Thackeray, smarting under the elaborate and unjust attack, portions of which were copied and widely circulated in other journals, could not but regard the friend and adviser of his critic as, in some degree, associated with it; and Mr. Dickens on the other hand, naturally hurt at finding his offer of arbitration rejected, gave the letters to the original author of the trouble for publication, with the remark—" As the receiver of my letter did not respect the confidence in which it addressed him, there can be none left for you to violate. I send you what I wrote to Mr. Thackeray, and what he wrote to me, and you are at perfect liberty to print the two." Thus, for a while, ended this painful affair. Readers of Disraeli's " Quarrels of Authors " will miss in it those sterner features of the dissensions between literary men as they were conducted in the old times; but none can contemplate this difference between the two great masters of fiction of our day with other than feelings of regret for the causes which led to it.

It is pleasing, however, to learn that the differences between them were ended before Mr. Thackeray's death. Singularly enough, this happy circumstance occurred only a few days before the time when it would have been too late. The two great authors met by accident in the lobby of a Club. They suddenly turned and saw each other, and the unrestrained impulse of both was to hold out the hand of forgiveness and fellowship. With that hearty grasp the difference which estranged them ceased for ever. This, says the narrator of this circumstance, must have been a great consolation to Mr. Dickens when he saw his great brother laid in the earth at Kensal Green; and no one who has read the beautiful and affecting article on Thackeray, from the hand of Mr. Dickens, just published in the "Cornhill Magazine," can doubt that all trace of this painful affair had vanished. We believe that the writer of the article which had created so much ill-will, when the angry feelings excited by these differences had passed away, was no less willing to admit that he had exceeded the limits of fair criticism, and, acting upon false impressions, had done an unintentional wrong.

CHAPTER V.

COMMENCEMENT OF THE "CORNHILL MAGAZINE"—UNSUCCESSFUL ATTEMPT AS A DRAMATIC WRITER—THE WOLF AND THE LAMB—THE MOUNTAIN SYLPH—THE ADVENTURES OF PHILIP—THE LECTURES ON THE GEORGES—EDITORIAL TROUBLES—ANECDOTES OF HIS CORRESPONDENTS—WITHDRAWAL FROM THE EDITORSHIP OF THE "CORNHILL"—BUILDING OF HIS HOUSE IN KENSINGTON PALACE GARDENS—MR. HANNAY'S ANECDOTES—DEATH OF MR. THACKERAY—CIRCUMSTANCES OF HIS ILLNESS—THE FUNERAL—HIS UNFINISHED WORK—MR. THACKERAY'S MANUSCRIPTS—HIS EARLY LIFE AT OTTERY ST. MARY—VERSES ON CATHOLIC EMANCIPATION MEETING—M. LOUIS BLANC'S LECTURES—MR. ROBERT BELL—SCENE AT LECTURE AT OXFORD—VARIOUS ANECDOTES—CONCLUSION.

THE great event of the last few years of Mr. Thackeray's life was the starting of the "Cornhill Magazine," the first Number of which, with the date of January, 1860, appeared shortly before Christmas in the previous year. The great success that Mr. Dickens had met with in conducting his weekly periodical, perhaps suggested to Messrs.

Smith, Elder, and Co. the project of their new monthly magazine, with Mr. Thackeray for editor. But few expected a design so bold and original as they found developed by the appearance of Number 1. The contents were by contributors of first-rate excellence; the quantity of matter in each was equal to that given by the old-established magazines, published at half-a-crown, while the price of the "Cornhill," as every one knows, was only a shilling. The editor's ideas on the subject of the new periodical were explained by him some weeks before the commencement in a characteristic letter to his friend, Mr. G. H. Lewes, which was afterwards adopted as the vehicle of announcing the design to the public.

"I am not mistaken," says this letter, "in supposing that my readers give me credit for experience and observation, for having lived with educated people in many countries, and seen the world in no small variety; and, having heard me soliloquize, with so much kindness and favour, and say my own say about life, and men and women, they will not be unwilling to try me as Conductor of a Concert, in which I trust many skilful performers will take part. We hope for a large number of readers, and must seek in the first place, to amuse and interest them. Fortunately for some folks, novels are as daily bread to others; and fiction of course must form a part, but only a part, of our entertainment. We want, on the other hand, as much reality as possible—discussion and narrative of events interesting to the public, personal adventures and observation, familiar reports of scientific discovery, description of Social Institutions—*quicquid agunt homines*—a Great Eastern, a Battle in China, a Race-Course, a popular Preacher—there is hardly any subject we *don't* want to hear about, from lettered and instructed men who are competent to speak on it."

The first number contained the commencement of that series of "Roundabout Papers," in which we get so many interesting glimpses of Mr. Thackeray's personal history and feelings, and also the opening chapters of his story of "Lovel the Widower." The latter was originally written in the form of a comedy, entitled "The Wolf and the Lamb," which was intended to be performed during the management of Mr. Wigan at the Olympic Theatre: but which was finally declined by the latter. Mr. Thackeray, we believe, acquiesced in the unfavourable judgment of the practical manager upon the acting qualities of his comedy; and resolved to throw it into narrative form in the story with which his readers are now familiar. This was not the first instance of his writing for the stage. If we are not mistaken, the libretto of Mr. John Barnett's popular opera of the "Mountain Sylph," produced some thirty years since, was from his pen. In the "Cornhill" also, appeared his story of "Philip on his way through the World." The scenes in this are said to have been founded in great part upon his own experiences; and there can be no doubt that the adventures of Philip Firmin represent, in many respects, those of the Charterhouse boy, who afterwards became known to the world as the author of "Vanity Fair." But in all such matters it is to be remembered that the writer of fiction feels himself at liberty to deviate from the facts of his life in any way which he finds necessary for the development of his story. Certainly the odious stepfather of Philip must not be taken for Mr. Thackeray's portrait of his own stepfather, towards whom he always entertained feelings of respect and affection. We may also remind our readers that the "Lectures on the Four Georges," first appeared in print in this popular periodical. The sales reached by the earlier numbers were enormous, and far beyond anything ever attained by a monthly magazine; even after the usual subsidence which follows the flush of a great success, the circulation had, we believe, settled at a point far exceeding the most sanguine hopes of the projectors.

These fortunate results of the undertaking were, however, not without serious drawbacks. The editor soon discovered that his new position was, in many respects, an unenviable one. Friends and acquaintances, not to speak of constant readers and "regular subscribers to your interesting magazine," sent him bushels of manuscripts, of which it was rare indeed to find one that could be accepted. Sensitive poets and poetesses took umbrage at refusals however kindly and delicately expressed. "How can I go into society with comfort?" asked the editor of a friend at this time. "I dined the other day at ——'s, and at the table were four gentlemen, whose masterpieces of literary art I had been compelled to decline with thanks." Not six months elapsed before he began to complain of "thorns" in the editorial cushion. One lady wrote to entreat that her article might be inserted on the ground that she had known better days, and had a sick and widowed mother to maintain—others began with fine phrases about the merits and eminent genius of the person they were addressing. Some found fault with articles, and abused contributor and editor. An Irishman threatened punishment for an implied libel in "Lovel the Widower," upon ballet-dancers, whom he declared to be superior to the snarlings of dyspeptic libellers, or the spiteful attacks and *brutum fulmen* of ephemeral authors. This gentleman also informed the editor that theatrical managers were in the habit of speaking good English—possibly better than ephemeral authors. "Out of mere malignity," exclaims the unfortunate editor, "I suppose there is no man who would like to make enemies. But here, in this editorial business you can't do otherwise; and a queer, strange, bitter thought it is that must cross the mind of many a public man. 'Do what I will, be innocent or spiteful, be generous or cruel, there are A. and B. and C. and D. who will hate me to the end of the chapter—to the chapter's end—to the finis of the page—when hate and envy, and fortune and disappointment shall be over.'"*

It was chiefly owing to these causes that Mr. Thackeray finally determined to withdraw from the editorship of the Magazine; though continuing to contribute to it, and to take an interest in its progress. In an amusing address to contributors and correspondents, dated 18th March, 1862, he announces this determination. "I believe," he says, "my own special readers will agree that my books will not suffer when their author is released from the daily task of reading, accepting, refusing, losing and finding the works of other people. To say 'No,' has often caused me a morning's peace, and a day's work. Oh, those hours of madness, spent in searching for Louisa's lost lines to her dead 'Piping Bullfinch,' or 'Nhoj Senoj's'† mislaid Essay. I tell them for the last time that the (late) Editor will not be responsible for rejected communications, and herewith send off the chair and the great " Cornhill Magazine "

* " Roundabout Papers," No. 5.
† The reader will discover the meaning of this by reversing the letters of Nhoj Senoj's name.

tin box with its load of care." In the same address he announced that while the tale of "Philip" had been passing through the press, he had been preparing another, on which he had worked at intervals for many years past, and which he hoped to introduce in the following year.

In a pecuniary sense, the "Cornhill Magazine" had undoubtedly proved a fortunate venture for its editor. It was during his editorship that he removed from his house, No. 36, Onslow-square, in which he had resided for some years, to the more congenial neighbourhood of the Palace at Kensington, that "Old Court Suburb," which Mr. Leigh Hunt has gossiped about so pleasantly. Mr. Thackeray took upon a long lease, a somewhat dilapidated mansion on the west side of Kensington Palace-gardens. His intention was to repair and improve it, but he finally resolved to pull it down, and build another in its stead. The new house, a handsome, solid mansion of choice red brick with stone facings, was built from a design drawn by himself; and in this house he continued to reside till the time of his death. "It was," says Mr. Hannay, "a dwelling worthy of one who really represented literature in the great world, and who planting himself on his books, yet sustained the character of his profession with all the dignity of a gentleman. A friend who called on him there from Edinburgh, in the summer of 1862, knowing of old his love of the Venusian, playfully reminded him what Horace says of those who, regardless of their sepulchre, employ themselves in building houses:—

"Sepulchri
Immemor struis domos."

"Nay," said he, "I am *memor sepulchri*, for this house will always let for so many hundreds (mentioning the sum) a year." We may add, that Mr. Thackeray was always of opinion, that notwithstanding the somewhat costly proceeding of pulling down and re-erecting, he had achieved the rare result for a private gentleman, of building for himself a house which, regarded as an investment of a portion of his fortune, left no cause for regret.

Our brief narrative draws to a close. The announcement of the death of Mr. Thackeray, coming so suddenly upon us in the very midst of our great Christian festival of 1863, created a sensation which will be long remembered. His hand had been missed in the last two numbers of the "Cornhill Magazine," but only because he had been busily engaged in laying the foundations of another of those continuous works of fiction which his readers so eagerly expected. In the then current Number of the "Cornhill Magazine," the customary orange-coloured fly-leaf had announced that 'a new serial story' by him would be commenced early in the new year; but the promise had scarcely gone abroad when we learnt that the hand which had penned its opening chapters, in the full prospect of a happy ending, could never again add line or word to that long range of writings which must always remain one of the best evidences of the strength and beauty of our English speech.

On the Tuesday preceding he had followed to the grave his relative, Lady Rodd, widow of Vice-Admiral Sir John Tremayne Rodd, K.C.B., who was the daughter of Major James Rennell, F.R.S., Surveyor-General of Bengal, by the daughter of the Rev. Dr. Thackeray, Head Master of Harrow

School. Only the day before this, according to a newspaper account, he had been congratulating himself on having finished four numbers of a new novel; he had the manuscript in his pocket, and with a boyish frankness showed the last pages to a friend, asking him to read them, and see what he could make of them. When he had completed four numbers more he said he would subject himself to the skill of a very clever surgeon, and be no more an invalid. Only two days before he had been seen at his club in high spirits; but with all his high spirits, he did not seem well; he complained of illness; but he was often ill, and he laughed off his present attack. He said that he was about to undergo some treatment which would work a perfect cure in his system, and so he made light of his malady. He was suffering from two distinct complaints, one of which has now wrought his death. More than a dozen years before, while he was writing "Pendennis," the publication of that work was stopped by his serious illness. He was brought to death's door, and he was saved from death by Dr. Elliotson, to whom, in gratitude, he dedicated the novel when he lived to finish it.

But ever since that ailment he had been subject every month or six weeks to attacks of sickness, attended with violent retching. He was con-gratulating himself, just before his death, on the failure of his old enemy to return, and then he checked himself, as if he ought not to be too sure of a release from his plague. On the morning of Wednesday, the 23rd of December, the complaint returned, and he was in great suffering all day.* He was no better in the evening, and his valet, Charles Sargent, left him at eleven o'clock on Wednesday night, Mr. Thackeray wishing him " Good night " as he went out of the room. At nine o'clock on the following morning the valet entering his master's chamber as usual, he found him lying on his back quite still, with his arms spread over the coverlet, but he took no notice, as he also was accustomed to see his master thus after one of his stomach attacks. He brought some coffee and set it down beside the bed, and it was only when he returned after an interval and found that the cup had not been tasted, that a sudden

* *Times* Newspaper, 25th Dec., 1863.

alarm seized him, and he discovered that his master was dead. About midnight Mr. Thackeray's mother, who slept overhead, had heard him get up and walk about his room; but she was not alarmed, as this was a habit of her son when unwell. It is supposed that he had, in fact, been seized at this time, and that the violence of the attack had brought on the effusion on the brain, which, as the *post-mortem* examination showed, was the immediate cause of death. His medical attendants attributed his death to effusion on the brain. They added that he had a very large brain, weighing no less than $58\frac{1}{2}$ oz. He thus died of the complaint which seemed to trouble him least.

The shock occasioned by the news of his death cannot be better described than in the words of one whose generous testimony is the more interesting from the fact of its author having been the acknowledged writer of the unjust and inconsiderate sketch of Mr. Thackeray's life and character, which had led to the unhappy dissensions in the Garrick Club.

"On Christmas-Eve," says Mr. Edmund Yates, the

writer referred to, "in the twilight, at the time when the clubs are filled with men who have dropped in on their homeward way to hear the latest news, or to exchange pleasant jests or seasonable greetings, a rumour ran through London that Thackeray was dead. I myself heard it on club steps from the friend who had just returned from telegraphing the intelligence to an Irish newspaper, and at first doubted, as all did, the authenticity of the information. One had seen him two days before, another had dined in his company but two nights previously; but it was true! Thackeray was dead; and the purest English prose writer of the nineteenth century, and the novelist with a greater knowledge of the human heart as it really is than any one—with the exception, perhaps, of Shakspeare and Balzac—was suddenly struck down in the midst of us. In the midst of us! No long illness, no lingering decay, no gradual suspension of power; almost pen in hand, like Kempenfelt, he went down. Well said the *Examiner*—'Whatever little feuds may have gathered about Mr. Thackeray's public life lay lightly on the surface of the minds that chanced to be in contest with him. They could be thrown off in a moment, at the first shock of the news that he was dead.' It seemed impossible to realize the fact. No other celebrity, be he writer, statesman, artist, actor, seemed so thoroughly a portion of London. That 'good grey head which all men knew' was as easy of recognition as his to whom the term applied, the Duke of Wellington. Scarcely a day passed without his being seen in the Pall-Mall districts; and a Londoner showing country cousins the wonders of the metropolis, generally knew how to arrange for them to have a sight of the great English writer. The *Examiner* was right. God knows! the shock had thrown off all but regretful feelings, and an impossibility to comprehend the magnitude of the sudden loss. We talked of him—of how, more than any other author, he had written about what is said of men immediately after their death—of how he had written of the death-chamber, 'They shall come in here for the last time to you, my friend in motley.' We read that marvellous sermon which the week-day preacher delivered to entranced thousands over old John Sedley's dead body, and 'sadly fell our Christmas-Eve.' One would have thought that the *Times* could have spared more space than a bare three-quarters of a column for the record of such a man's life and death. One would have thought that Westminster Abbey might have opened her doors for the reception of the earthly remains of one whose name will echo to the end of time. And, as I write, the thought occurs to me that the same man was, perhaps, the last to wish for either of such distinctions."

The funeral took place on the 30th of December, the body being interred in Kensal Green cemetery. The day was beautiful, and the atmosphere as balmy as if it were June instead of December. On the way to the cemetery there could be seen not only the carriages of the aristocratic and wealthy, but also many persons of the humbler class; and, indeed, there was much evidence at the grave that the English people— and not any particular class—felt their bereavement in the gifted and genial author. It was remarkable also what various departments of life and thought were represented—the actor and the artist, the editor and the novelist, the poet and the clergyman, all were there to mourn over one whose mind and heart were a hundred-gated city. Amongst the 1500 persons present were noticed Mr. Robert Browning, Mr. Charles Dickens, Mr. Anthony Trollope, Mr. Mark Lemon, Mr. G. H. Lewes, Mr. Theodore Martin, Mr. Isaac Butt, M.P., Mr. W. H. Russell, LL.D., Mr. Laurence, barrister; Mr. J. C. O'Dowd, barrister; Mr. Higgins (Jacob Omnium), Mr. Robert Bell, Mr. Howell Morgan, the High Sheriff of Merionethshire; Rev. Dr. Rudge, the Archdeacon of London, Master of the Charterhouse, in which Mr. Thackeray was educated; Mr. Millais, R.A.; Mr. George Cruikshank, an old friend of Mr. Thackeray, with whom in his early life the author studied etching; Mr. Leech, Mr. Shirley Brooks,

Mr. Creswell, Mr. H. Cole, C.B., Mr. C. L. Gruneisen, Mr. Charles Mathews, Mr. Tom Taylor, Sir J. Carmichael, Mr. J. Hollingshead, Mr. Dallas, Mr. O'Neile, Mr. Creswick, R.A.; M. Louis Blanc, Mr. Walker, Mr. E. Piggott, Mr. M. D. Conway, Mr. G. J. Holyoake, and Miss Braddon. Mr. Carlyle, between whom and Mr. Thackeray a friendship of many years subsisted, was prevented from attending by illness in his family.

The funeral procession, which, in accordance with the well-known tastes of the deceased, was remarkably simple, arrived at the cemetery about twelve o'clock. There was but one mourning coach, in which were seated Mr. F. St. John Thackeray and Mr. James Rodd, cousins of the deceased. In the succeeding carriage, the private carriage of Mr. Thackeray, were Captain Shaw, his brother-in-law, and the Hon. E. Curzon. The remaining coaches were those of Earl Granville, Mr. Martin Thackeray, General Low, Lord Gardiner, Sir W. Fraser, Hon. E. Curzon, Mr. Macaulay, Q.C., Sir James Colville, and Mr. Bradbury, of the eminent publishing firm of Bradbury and Evans.

The funeral service was read by the chaplain of the cemetery, Rev. Charles Stuart.

The Misses Thackeray were present in the chapel, and also looked into the grave. A deep sympathy was felt by all in their profound grief at the loss of one whose tenderness as a man was not less than his strength as an author.

The coffin was quite plain and bore the inscription :—

WILLIAM MAKEPEACE THACKERAY, ESQ.,
DIED 24TH DECEMBER, 1863,
AGED 52 YEARS.

The scene was altogether deeply impressive. Many eyes were fastened upon Mr. Dickens, as he stood, side by side with Mr. Browning, looking into the grave of one whose greatness none could or did more appreciate. But there were many unknown to fame, and whose ties to the deceased were known only to their own hearts, who pressed their way to gaze with evident sorrow on the coffin. And after the solemn words, " dust to dust " had fallen on the sad hearts there gathered, and the ceremonies were over, the company seemed loth to depart, and lingered in quiet and hushed conversation around the grave.

Just before his death, as has been already stated, he had rejoiced over the completion of the fourth monthly portion of his story, seeing in it the promise of a work which would not be found, when completed, to fall short even of his fame. It was, like the Virginians, a story of the times of George the First and George the Second. Some months previously it was rumoured that the next work from his pen would relate to an early period of English history—a statement which a bold guesser subsequently enlarged into the assertion that its scene would be laid in the times of the Anglo-Saxons. Its author was doubtless amused at the paragraphs which made the customary tour through the press of London and the provinces, gravely informing the world that the author of "Esmond," and the "Essays on the Humourists," who had hitherto delighted in the times of elaborate flowing wigs, and swords, and coats with huge lapels, had suddenly betaken himself to those misty days of savage manners and scanty clothing. The rumour, in its unembellished form was, however, not without foundation. He had recently contemplated writing a story of the days of Henry the Fifth, in which period of our history some accidental bent of his reading had led him to take a special interest. He had even thought of some of its details, and had amused himself in imagination with a grotesque scene in one of the old chroniclers of a famous royal lady, who rode into a fair city of Normandy upon a cow. But the notion was laid aside. His old passion for re-creating the life and manners of the last century was too powerful to be resisted, and he finally found himself at home in a story of English life of the old period, in which the elaborate imitation of the style of the Augustan age would not be allowed, as in the "Adventures of Henry Esmond," to interfere with the development of a story of a good and heroic stamp, in the presence of which the old complaints from adverse critics of cynicism and coldness should be heard no more.

SOME few detached anecdotes may here be added. Mr. Thackeray was remarkable among his fellow literary men no less for the clearness of his handwriting than for the general neatness of his manuscripts. Page after page of that small round hand would be written by him absolutely—for he rarely altered his first draughts in any way—without interlineation, blot, or blemish of any kind. Only a few weeks before he died he spent a morning in the reading-room of the British Museum, and there by accident left upon a table a page of the manuscript of his unpublished story. The paper being found by the attendant, so well was this fact known, that the extreme clearness of the writing at once suggested its owner. An appeal to one of the officials who was familiar with his autographs decided the matter, and Mr. Thackeray, to his great surprise and gratification, was interrupted in his fruitless search at home by the arrival of a letter enclosing the missing page.

It having been stated in an Exeter paper that Mr. Thackeray, when a boy, went to school at Ottery St. Mary, in that county, the Rev. Dr.

Cornish, the vicar of that place, has recently
written to contradict it. It appears from the
Doctor's letter that the step-father of the great
novelist rented an estate near Ottery St. Mary,
and that the latter, while stopping there, used to
visit at the vicarage and borrow books of Dr.
Cornish. The scenery of Clavering St. Mary and
Chatteris, in " Pendennis," corresponds, according
to the latter, in minute particulars with that of
Ottery St. Mary and Exeter. One of the little
marginal vignettes in that famous novel is a picture of the clock tower of Ottery church. Thackeray describes the youthful Pendennis as galloping
through " the Iliad and Odyssey, the tragic play-
writers, and the charming wicked Aristophanes,
whom he vowed to be the greatest poet of all."
When the author was about the age of his young
hero, he borrowed of Dr. Cornish Carey's translation of " The Birds of Aristophanes," which he
read, says the Doctor, with intense delight, and
returned it with three humorous illustrative drawings. Mr. Thackeray says in " Pendennis "—
" It was at this period of his existence that Pen
broke out in the poet's corner of the county

Chronicle with some verses with which he was perfectly well satisfied." Dr. Cornish adds that when the great Catholic emancipation meeting took place on Penenden Heath, Thackeray brought him some verses, which were afterwards forwarded to an Exeter paper for insertion, and duly appeared. These verses, the Doctor thinks, were the first composition of the great humourist that were ever published:—

IRISH MELODY.
Air—" The Minstrel Boy."

Mister Shiel into Kent has gone,
   On Penenden Heath you'll find him;
Nor think you that he came alone,
   There's Doctor Doyle behind him.
"Men of Kent," said this little man,
   " If you hate Emancipation,
You're a set of fools:" he then began
   A " cut and dry " oration.

He strove to speak, but the men of Kent,
   Began a grievous shouting,
When out of his waggon the little man went,
   And put a stop to his spouting.
" What though these heretics heard me not,"
   Quoth he to his friend Canonical;
" My speech is safe in the *Times* I wot,
   And eke in the *Morning Chronicle*."

Louis Blanc, the historian of the French Revolution, has recently related in a French newspaper the following story:—"A few years ago the London papers announced that a Frenchman whose name I need not give you [M. Louis Blanc], was going to deliver in English what is here called a lecture. Foremost among those who were moved by a feeling of a delicate kindness and hospitable curiosity to encourage the lecturer with their presence was Thackeray. When the lecture was over, the manager of the literary institution where it was delivered, for some reason or other, recommended the company to take care of their pockets in the crowd at the doors—a hint which was not particularly to the taste of a highly respectable and even distinguished audience. Some even protested, and none more warmly than an unknown person, very well dressed, sitting next to Mr. Robert Bell. Not content with speaking, this unknown person gesticulated in a singularly animated manner. 'Isn't such a suggestion indecent, sir, insulting?' said he to Mr. Bell. 'What does he take us for?' &c., &c. After giving vent to his indignation in this way for some moments, the susceptible stranger disappeared, and when Mr. Robert Bell, who wanted to know how long the lecture had lasted, put his hand to his watch-pocket, behold! his watch had disappeared likewise. Thackeray, to whom his excellent friend mentioned the mishap, invited Robert Bell to dinner a day or two after. When the day came, Robert Bell took his seat at his friend's table, round which a joyous company of wits were gathered, and soon found himself encircled by a rattling fire of banter about an article of his which had just appeared in the 'Cornhill Magazine,' then conducted by Thackeray; an article remarkable in all respects, and which had attracted universal notice, as a faithful, serious, and philosophical account of some effects of *Spiritism* which the author had witnessed at a *séance* given by Mr. Home. Mr. Robert Bell is an admirable *causeur;* his talk is a happy mixture of an Englishman's good sense and an Irishman's *verve.* So his questioners found their match in brilliant fence. Next day a mysterious messenger arrived at Mr. Robert Bell's, and handed to him, without saying who had sent it, a box containing a note, worded, as nearly as I recollect, as follows:

—'The Spirits present their compliments to Mr. Robert Bell, and as a mark of their gratitude to him, they have the honour to return him the watch that was stolen from him.' And a watch it really was that the box contained, but a watch far finer and richer than the one which had disappeared. Mr. Robert Bell at once thought of Thackeray, and wrote to him without further explanation:—'I don't know if it is you, but it is very like you.' Thackeray in reply sent a caricature portrait of himself, drawn by his own hand, and representing a winged spirit in a flowing robe, and spectacles on nose. Thackeray had in early life taken to painting, and perhaps if he had pursued his first vocation, he might have come in time to handle the brush as well as he afterwards handled the pen. At any rate the drawing in question, as I can bear witness, was one to bring tears into your eyes for laughing. It was accompanied by a note as follows:—'The Spirit Gabriel presents his compliments to Mr. Robert Bell, and takes the liberty to communicate to him the portrait of the person who stole the watch.' Now, is not this bit of a story charming? What grace!

what delicacy! what humour in this inspiration of a friend who, to punish his friend for having done the Spirits the honour to speak of them, sends him with a smile a magnificent present. Honourable to Thackeray, this anecdote is equally so to Robert Bell, who could inspire such feelings in such a man. And this is why I feel a double pleasure in relating it."

AN anonymous writer says:—" The first time I heard Mr. Thackeray read in public, he paid a tribute to 'Boz.' It was the night after the Oxford election, in which Mr. Thackeray was an unsuccessful candidate, and the kind-hearted author hastened up to town to fulfil a promise to give some readings on behalf of Mr. Angus Reach.* I well remember the burst of laughter and applause which greeted the opening words of his reading. ' Walking yesterday down the streets of an ancient and well-known city, I,'—but here the allusion to Oxford was recognized, and he had to wait until

---

* The writer is here in error. The Lecture was not delivered on behalf of Mr. Reach, but for the fund then being raised to the memory of the late Douglas Jerrold.

the merriment it created had ceased. In alluding to Charles Dickens, Mr. Thackeray, after speaking with abhorrence of the impurity of the writings of Sterne, went on to say :—' The foul satyr's eyes leer out of the leaves constantly ; the last words the famous author wrote were bad and wicked— the last lines the poor stricken wretch penned were for pity and pardon. I think of these past writers, and of one who lives amongst us now, and am grateful for the innocent laughter and the sweet and unsullied pages which the author of ' David Copperfield ' gives to my children.' The author of ' David Copperfield ' was taken by surprise, and looked immensely hard at the ceiling, as if trying to persuade himself that he was unknown to the audience. On the same night I heard Thackeray read Hood's celebrated lines, ' One more unfortunate,' &c."

THE same writer observes :—" Thackeray was a member of the Reform, the Athenæum, and the Garrick Clubs—perhaps of others, but it was in those I have named that his leisure was usually spent. The afternoons of the last week of his life were almost entirely passed at the Reform Club, and never had he been more genial or in such apparently happy moods. Many men sitting in the libraries and the dining rooms of these Clubs, have thought this week of one of the tenderest passages in his early sketches—'Brown the younger at a Club,'—in which the old uncle is represented as telling his nephew, while showing him the various rooms of the club, of those who had dropped off—whose names had appeared at the end of the Club list, under the dismal category of 'members deceased,' in which (added Thackeray) 'You and I shall rank some day.'"

MR. HANNAY says "his frankness and *bonhommie* made him delightful in a *tête-à-tête*, and gave a pleasant human flavour to talk full of sense, and wisdom, and experience, and lighted up by the gaiety of the true London man of the world. Though he said witty things, now and then, he was not a wit in the sense in which Jerrold was, and he complained, sometimes, that his best things occurred to him after the occasion had gone by! He shone most—as in his books—

in little subtle remarks on life, and little descriptive sketches suggested by the talk. We remember, in particular, one evening, after a dinner-party at his house, a fancy picture he drew of Shakspeare during his last years at Stratford, sitting out in the summer afternoon watching the people, which all who heard it, brief as it was, thought equal to the best things in his Lectures. But it was not for this sort of talent,—rarely exerted by him,—that people admired his conversation. They admired, above all, the broad sagacity, sharp insight, large and tolerant liberality, which marked him as one who was a sage as well as a story-teller, and whose stories were valuable because he was a sage. Another point of likeness to him in Scott was that he never over-valued story-telling, or forgot that there were nobler things in literature than the purest creation of which the object was amusement." *

* Mr. Hannay's interesting sketch, originally published in the form of an article in the *Edinburgh Courant*, has since been reprinted in a pamphlet form by Messrs. Oliver and Boyd, of Edinburgh.

THACKERAY and FIELDING.—Thackeray, many years since, came down into Somersetshire to visit some friends in the bright and sunny days of Sydney Smith, and rejoiced in the society and cordial hospitality of the witty Rector of Combe Florey. Unfortunately, there is no Boswell to record the good things uttered by these noble humourists. Thackeray, at a later period of his life, contemplated a pilgrimage to Sharpham Park, near Glastonbury, the birth-place of Fielding, whose character he has drawn with such genuine sympathy and discernment in his " Lectures on the English Humourists." He was gratified to learn from a gentleman living in that part of the country, Mr. Kinglake, that a place in the Gallery of "West Country" Worthies, with the glorious company of Blake and Locke, was reserved for the author of " Tom Jones." The inscription for the Fielding Memorial would have been the work of Mr. Thackeray's hand if his life had been spared a few months longer. He was fond of repeating Gibbons' panegyric on Fielding. It is as follows :—" Our immortal Fielding was of the younger branch of the Earls of Denbigh, who drew their origin from the Counts of Hapsburg. The successors of Charles V. may disdain their brethren of England, but the romance of 'Tom Jones,' that exquisite picture of human manners, will outlive the Palace of the Escurial, and the Imperial Eagle of Austria."

IN October, 1855, a dinner was given to Mr. Thackeray at the London Tavern, of which one who was present gave at the time the following account:—"The Thackeray dinner was a triumph. Covers, we are assured, were laid for sixty; and sixty and no more sat down precisely at the minute named to do honor to the great novelist. Sixty very hearty shakes of the hand did Thackeray receive from sixty friends on that occasion; and hearty cheers from sixty vociferous and friendly tongues followed the chairman's, Mr. Charles Dickens, proposal of his health, and of wishes for his speedy and successful return among us. Dickens—the best after-dinner speaker now alive—was never happier. He spoke as if he was fully conscious that it was a great occasion, and that the absence of even one reporter was a matter of congratulation, affording ampler room to unbend. The table was in the shape of a horseshoe, having two vice-chairmen; and this circumstance was wrought up and played with by Dickens in the true Sam Weller and Charles Dickens manner. Thackeray, who is far from what is called a good speaker, outdid himself. There was his usual hesitation; but this hesitation becomes his manner of speaking and his matter, and is never unpleasant to his hearers, though it is, we are assured, most irksome to himself. This speech was full of pathos, and humour, and oddity, with bits of prepared parts imperfectly recollected, but most happily made good by the felicities of the passing moment. Like the 'Last Minstrel,'

'Each blank in faithless memory void
The poet's glowing thought supplied.'

It was a speech to remember for its earnestness of purpose and its undoubted originality. Then the chairman quitted, and many near and at a distance, quitted with him. Thackeray was on the move with the chairman, when, inspired by the moment, Jerrold took the chair, and

Thackeray remained. Who is to chronicle what now passed?—what passages of wit—what neat and pleasant sarcastic speeches in proposing healths—what varied and pleasant, ay, and at times, sarcastic acknowledgments? Up to the time when Dickens left, a good reporter might have given all, and with ease, to future ages: but there could be no reporting what followed. There were words too nimble and too full of flame for a dozen Gurneys, all ears, to catch and preserve. Few will forget that night. There was an 'air of wit' about the room for three days after. Enough to make the two next companies, though downright fools, right witty."

MR. SHIRLEY BROOKS has given an interesting account of the last occasion on which he saw Mr. Thackeray. It was at the Garrick Club, on Wednesday the 16th of December. Mr. Thackeray, who was dining, was, he tells us, in his usual spirits, which were never boisterous and always cheerful, and he had pleasant words for all present. "On that evening," adds Mr. Brooks, "he enjoyed himself much, in his own quiet way, and contributed genially to the enjoyment of those who were something less quiet; and, a question arising about a subscription in aid of a disabled artist, he instantly offered to increase, if necessary, a sum he had previously promised. The writer's very last recollection of the 'cynic,' therefore, is in connexion with an unasked act of Christian kindness. On the following Monday he attended the funeral of a lady who was interred in Kensal Green Cemetery. On the Tuesday evening he came to his favourite club—the Garrick—and asked a seat at the table of two friends, who, of course, welcomed him as all welcomed Thackeray. It will not be deemed too minute a record by any of the hundreds who personally loved him to note where he sat for the last time in that club. There is in the dining-room on the first floor a nook near the reading room. The principal picture hanging in that nook, and fronting you as you approach it, is the celebrated one from 'The Clandestine Marriage,' with Lord Ogleby, Canton, and Brush. Opposite to that Thackeray took his seat and dined with his friends. He was afterwards in the smoking room, a place in which he delighted. The Garrick Club will remove in a few months, and all these details will be nothing to its new members, but much to many of its old ones. His place there will know him and them no more. On the Wednesday he was out several times, and was seen in Palace Gardens 'reading a book.' Before the dawn on Thursday, he was where there is no night."

To the information concerning Mr. Thackeray's family which we have already given, we may add the following particulars. Dr. George Thackeray, an uncle, we believe, of the deceased author, was provost of King's from 1814 till his death in 1850, the very dignity which, as our readers will remember, the good Dr. Thomas Thackeray, the novelist's great grandfather, had unsuccessfully competed for. Another connexion, the Rev. Mr. Thackeray, was instituted by King's College to a living in Norfolk in 1846, and another to a living in Lincolnshire in 1840. Six members of the family took their degrees at Cambridge from different colleges in the interval between 1800 and 1823, and eight more Thackerays stand in the list of Cambridge graduates between 1685 and the end of the last century. A cousin of the deceased, a first-class man, and late fellow of Lincoln College, Oxford, is now one of the assistant-masters at Eton; and another cousin, Lieutenant Edward Talbot Thackeray, of the Bengal Engineers, obtained, in 1862, the Victoria Cross in reward for his cool intrepidity and daring in extinguishing a fire in the Delhi magazine inclosure on the 16th September, 1857, under a heavy fire from the enemy, at the imminent risk of his life from an explosion.

To his intimate friends, it must be pleasing to see how much progress has been made, even in the brief period which has elapsed since his death, towards a right appreciation of his character. The notion that the man, who with such delicate irony and unsparing satire laid bare the folly and wickedness of "Vanity Fair," must necessarily be harsh and misanthropical, is already forgotten. Men remember now the many eloquent and tender passages in which he touches upon human frailty, or depicts the brighter side of life, the many noble appeals which he has made in favour of charity and forbearance. Nor is this entirely due to our natural tenderness towards those who have just passed through that dark and narrow gateway whither all human footsteps tend. For some time past, these truer ideas of his private character have been gaining ground. It is said that of late, and since the one great over-shadowing affliction of his domestic life had been softened down, nothing had caused him so much pain as his sense that his satirical writings had led many to regard him as a heartless cynic. It was natural that he should strive to remove this impression; but the proofs of his good-heartedness are too numerous, and many of too old a date, as in his kindness to Maginn, to Louis Marvy and others, to be attributed to this cause. One of the newspaper reporters, in describing the funeral, touchingly remarks that some persons took a farewell sorrowful look into his grave, who were not recognized there among the great assemblage of literary and artistic celebrities, and whose bond of sympathy or ground of gratitude towards the deceased were known only to themselves. To those who knew best his private life this will be most intelligible. Time will assuredly do justice to his memory.

MR. THACKERAY'S PUBLIC SPEECHES:

A Selection from Notes taken on various occasions.

THE peculiar humour of Mr. Thackeray is nowhere more readily discernible than in his speeches. These were always unstudied, as the occasions when they were uttered allowed that freedom of fancy, and play of sudden thought, of which the pen is not always willing to make use. As such it is believed that these specimens of his public speaking, hitherto uncollected, will be welcome to his admirers.

LITERATURE *versus* POLITICS.
1848.

"If the approbation which my profession receives is such as Mr. Adolphus is pleased to say it has been [he had just been speaking of the very high importance of this branch of literature, and of Mr. Thackeray as one of its most distinguished ornaments], I can only say that we are nearly as happy in this country as our brother literary men are in foreign countries; and that we have all but arrived at the state of dethroning you all. I don't wish that this catastrophe should be brought about for the sake of personal quiet; for one, I am desirous to read my books, write my articles, and get

my money. I don't wish that that should take
place; but if I survey mankind, not 'from China
to Peru,' but over the map of Europe, with that
cursory glance which novel-writers can afford to
take, I see nothing but literary men who seem
to be superintending the affairs of the Continent,
and only our happy island which is exempt from
the literary despotism. Look to Italy, towards
the boot of which I turn my eyes, and first, I
find that a great number of novelists and literary
men are *bouleversing* the country from toe to
heel, turning about Naples, and kicking Rome
here and there, and causing a sudden onward
impetus of the monarchy of the great Carlo Alberto himself. If I go to France, I find that men,
and more particularly men of my own profession
and Mr. James's profession, are governing the
country; I find that writers of fiction and authors
in general are ruling over the destinies of the
empire; that Pegasus is, as it were, the charger
of the first citizen of the Republic. But arriving
at my own country. I beseech you to remember
that there was a time, a little time ago, on the
'10th of April last,' when a great novelist—a
great member of my own profession—was standing upon Kennington Common in the van of
liberty, prepared to assume any responsibility, to
take upon himself any direction of government,
to decorate himself with the tricolour sash, or the
Robespierre waistcoat; and but for the timely,

and I may say 'special' interposition of many who are here present, you might have been at present commanded by a president of a literary republic, instead of by our present sovereign. I doubt whether any presidents of any literary republics would contribute as much to the funds of this society. I don't believe that the country as yet requires so much of our literary men; but in the meanwhile I suppose it must be the task and endeavour of all us light practitioners of literature to do our best, to say our little say in the honestest way we can, to tell the truth as heartily and as simply as we are able to tell it, to expose the humbug, and to support the honest man."

THE REALITY OF THE NOVELIST'S CREATION.
1849.

"I suppose, Mr. Chairman, years ago when you had a duty to perform, you did not think much about, or look to, what men of genius and men of eloquence in England might say of you; but you went and you did your best with all your power, and what was the result? You determined to do your best on the next occasion. I believe that is the philosophy of what I have been doing in the course of my life; I don't know whether it has tended to fame or to laughter, or to seriousness; but I have tried to say the truth, and as far as I know, I have tried to describe what I saw before me, as well as I best might, and to like my neighbour as well as my neighbour would let me like him. All the rest of the speech which I had prepared, has fled into thin air; the only part of it which I remember was an apology for, or rather, an encomium of, the profession of us novelists, which, I am bound to say, for the honour of our calling, ought to rank with the very greatest literary occupations. Why should historians take precedence of us? Our personages are as real as theirs. For instance, I maintain that our friends Parson Adams and Dr. Primrose are characters as authentic as Dr. Sacheverell, or Dr. Warburton, or any reverend personage of their times. Gil Blas is quite as real and as good a man as the Duke of Lerma, and, I believe, a great deal more so. I was thinking too, that Don Quixote was to my mind as real a man as Don John or the Duke of Alva; and then I was turning to the history of a gentleman of whom I am particularly fond—a schoolfellow of mine before Dr. RUSSELL's time. I was turning to the life and history of one with whom we are all acquainted, and that is one Mr. Joseph Addison, who, I remember, was made Under-Secretary of State at one period of his life, under another celebrated man, Sir Charles Hedges, I think it was, but it is now so long ago, I am not sure; but I have no doubt Mr. Addison was much more proud of his connexion with Sir Charles Hedges, and his place in Downing-street, and his red box, and his quarter's salary, punctually and regularly paid; I dare say he was much more proud of these, than of any literary honour which he received, such as being the author of the 'Tour to Italy,' and the 'Campaign.' But after all, though he was indubitably connected with Sir Charles Hedges, there was another knight with whom he was much more connected, and that was a certain Sir Roger de Coverley, whom we have always loved, and believed in a thousand times better than a thousand Sir Charles Hedges. And as I look round at this my table, gentlemen, I cannot but perceive that the materials for my favourite romances are never likely to be wanting to future authors. I don't know that anything I have written has been generally romantic; but if I were disposed to write a romance, I think I should like to try an Indian tale, and I should take for the heroes of it, or for some of the heroes of it—I would take the noble lord whom I see opposite to me [Lord Napier] with the Sutlej flowing before him, and the enemy in his front, and himself riding before the British army, with his little son Arthur and his son Charles by his side. I am sure, in all the regions of romance, I could find nothing more noble and affecting than that story, and I hope some of these days, some more able novelist will undertake it."

AUTHORS AND THEIR PATRONS.
1851.

"Literary men are not by any means, at this present time, that most unfortunate and most degraded set of people whom they are sometimes represented to be. If foreign gentlemen should by any chance go to see 'The Rivals' represented at one of our theatres, they will see Captain Absolute and Miss Lydia Languish making love to one another, and conversing, if not in the costume of our present day, or such as gentlemen and ladies are accustomed to use, at any rate in something near it; whereas, when the old father Sir Anthony Absolute comes in, nothing will content the stage but that he should appear with red heels, large buckles, and an immense Ramilies wig. This is the stage tradition: they won't believe in an old man, unless he appears in this dress, and with this wig; nor in an old lady, unless she comes forward in a quilted petticoat and high-heeled shoes; nor in Hamlet's gravedigger, unless he wears some four-and-twenty waistcoats; and so on. In my trade, in my especial branch of literature, the same tradition exists; and certain persons are constantly apt to bring forward, or to believe in the existence at this moment, of the miserable old literary hack of the time of George the Second, and bring him before us as the literary man of this day. I say that that disreputable old phantom ought to be hissed out of society. I don't believe in the literary man being obliged to resort to ignoble artifices and mean flatteries, to get places at the tables of the great, and to enter into society upon sufferance. I don't believe in the patrons of this present day, except such patrons as I am happy to have in you, and as any honest man might be proud to have, and shake by the hand, and be shaken by the hand by. Therefore I propose from this day forward, that the oppressed literary man should disappear from among us. The times are altered; the people don't exist; 'the patron and the jail,' praise God, are vanished from out our institutions. It may be possible that the eminent Mr. Edmund Curl stood in the pillory in the time of Queen Anne, who, thank God, is dead; it may be, that in the reign of another celebrated monarch of these realms, Queen Elizabeth, authors who abused the persons of honours, would have their arms cut off on the first offence, and be hanged on the second. Gentlemen, what would be the position of my august friend and patron, Mr. Punch, if that were now the case? Where would be his hands, and his neck, and his ears, and his bowels? He would be disembowelled and his members cast about the land. We don't want patrons, we want friends; and I thank God, we have them. And as for any idea that our calling is despised by the world, I do for my part protest against and deny the whole statement. I have been in all sorts of society in this world, and I never have been despised that I know of. I don't believe there has been a literary man of the slightest merit, or of the slightest mark, who did not greatly advance himself by his literary labours. I see along this august table gentlemen whom I have had the honour of shaking by the hand and gentlemen whom I never should have called my friends, but for the humble literary labours I have been engaged in. And, therefore, I say, don't let us be pitied any more. As for pity being employed upon authors, especially in my branch of the profession, if you will but look at the novelists of the present day, I think you will see it is altogether out of the question to pity them. We will take in the first place, if you please, a great novelist who is the great head of a great party in a great assembly in this country. When this celebrated man went into his county to be proposed to represent it, and he was asked on what interest he stood? he nobly said, 'he stood on his *head*.' And who can question the gallantry and brilliancy of that eminent crest of his, and what man will deny the great merit of Mr. Disraeli? Take next another novelist, who writes from his ancestral hall, and addresses John Bull in letters on matters of politics, and John Bull buys eight editions of those letters. Is not this a prospect for a novelist? There is a third, who is employed upon this very evening, heart and hand, heart and voice, I may say, on a work of charity. And what is the consequence? The Queen of the realm, the greatest nobles of the empire, all the great of the world, will assemble to see him and do him honour. I say, therefore, don't let us have pity. I don't want it till I really *do* want it. Of course it is impossible for us to settle the mere prices by which the works of those who amuse the public are to be paid. I am perfectly aware that Signor Twankeydillo, of the Italian Opera, and Mademoiselle Petitpas, of the Haymarket, will get a great deal more money in a week, for the skilful exercise of their chest and toes, than I, or you, or any gentleman, shall be able to get by our brains and by weeks of hard labour. We cannot help these differences in payment, we know there must be high and low payments in our trade as in all trades; that there must be gluts of the market, and over production; that there must be successful machinery, and rivals, and brilliant importations from foreign countries; that there must be hands out of employ, and tribulation of workmen. But these ill winds which afflict us, blow fortunes to our successors. These are natural evils. It is the progress of the world, rather than any evil which we can remedy, and that is why I say this society acts most wisely and justly in endeavouring to remedy, not the chronic distress, but the temporary evil; that it finds a man at the moment of the pinch of necessity, helps him a little, and gives him a 'God speed,' and sends him on his way. For my own part I have felt that necessity, and bent under that calamity ; and it is because I have found friends who have nobly, with God's blessing, helped me at that moment of distress, that I feel deeply interested in the ends of a Society,* which has for its object to help my brethren in similar need."

THE NOVELIST'S FUTURE LABOURS.

1852.

"We, from this end of the table [on occasion of the Royal Literary Fund dinner], speak humbly and from afar off. We are the usefuls of the company, who over and over again perform our little part, deliver our little messages, and then sit down ; whereas you, yonder, are the great stars of the evening ;—you are collected with much care, and skill, and ingenuity, by the manager of this benefit performance ; you perform Macbeth and Hamlet, we are the Rozencrantzes and Guildensterns ; we are the Banquos,—as I know a Banquo who has shaken his gory old wig at Drury Lane, at a dozen Macbeths. We resemble the individual in plush, whom gentlemen may have seen at the Opera, who comes forward and demurely waters the stage, to the applause of the audience—never mind who is the great Taglioni, or the Lind, or the Wagner, who is to receive all

* Royal Literary Fund.

the glory. For my part, I am happy to fulfil that humble office, and to make my little spurt, and to retire, and leave the place for a greater and more able performer. How like British charity is to British valour! It always must be well fed before it comes into action! We see before us a ceremony of this sort, which Britons always undergo with pleasure. There is no tax which the Briton pays so cheerfully as the dinner-tax. Every man here, I have no doubt, who is a little acquainted with the world, must have received, in the course of the last month, a basketful of tickets, inviting him to meet in this place, for some purpose or other. We have all rapped upon this table, either admiring the speaker for his eloquence, or, at any rate, applauding him when he sits down. We all of us know—we have had it a hundred times—the celebrated flavour of the old Freemasons' mock-turtle, and the celebrated Freemasons' sherry; and if I seem to laugh at the usage, the honest, good old English usage, of eating and drinking, which brings us all together, for all sorts of good purposes—do not suppose that I laugh at it any more than I would at good, old, honest John Bull, who has under his good, huge, boisterous exterior, a great deal of kindness and goodness at the heart of him. Our festival may be compared with such a person; men meet here and shake hands, kind hearts grow kinder over the table, and a silent almoner issues forth from it, the festival over, and gratifies poor people, and relieves the suffering of the poor, which would never be relieved but for your kindness. So that there is a grace that follows after your meat and sanctifies it. We have heard the historians and their calling worthily exalted just now; but it seems to me that my calling will be the very longest and the last of those of all the literary gentlemen I see before me. Long after the present generation is dead—of readers and of authors of books—there must be kindness and generosity, and folly and fidelity, and love and heroism, and humbug in the world; and, as long as they last, my successors, or the successors of the novelists who come long after us, will have plenty to do, and plenty of subjects to write upon. There may chance to be a time when wars will be over, and the 'decisive battles' of the world will not need a historian. There may arrive a time when the Court of Chancery itself will be extinguished; and, as perhaps your Lordship is aware, there is a certain author of a certain work called 'Bleak House,' who, for the past three months, has been assaulting the Court of Chancery in a manner that I cannot conceive that ancient institution will survive. There may be a time when the Court of Chancery will cease to exist, and when the historian of the 'Lives of the Lord Chancellors' will have no calling. I have often speculated upon what the successors of the

Novelists in future ages may have to do; and I have fancied them occupied with the times and people of our own age. If I could fancy a man so occupied hereafter, and busied we will say with a heroic story, I would take the story which I heard hinted at the other night by the honoured, the oldest, the bravest and greatest man in this country—I would take the great and glorious action of Cape Danger, when, striking to the powers above alone, the Birkenhead went down! When, with heroic courage and endurance, the men remained on the decks, and the women and children were allowed to go away safe, as the people cheered them, and died doing their duty! I know of no victory so sublime in any annals of the feats of English valour—I know of no story that could inspire a great author or novelist better than that. Or, suppose we should take the story of an individual of the present day, whose name has been already mentioned; we might have a literary hero, not less literary than Mr. David Copperfield, or Mr. Arthur Pendennis, who is defunct: we might have a literary hero who, at twenty years of age, astonished the world with his brilliant story of 'Vivian Grey;' who, in a little time afterwards, and still in the youthful period of his life, amazed and delighted the public with 'The Wondrous Tale of Alroy;' who, presently following up the course of his career, and the development of his philosophical culture, explained to a breathless and listening world the great Caucasian mystery; who, quitting literature, then went into politics; met, faced, and fought, and conquered the great political giant, and great orator of those days; who subsequently led thanes and earls to battle, and caused reluctant squires to carry his lance; and who, but the other day, went in a gold coat to kiss the hand of his Sovereign, as Leader of the House of Commons and Chancellor of Her Majesty's Exchequer. What a hero that will be for some future novelist, and what a magnificent climax for the third volume of his story!"

COMMERCE AND LITERATURE.
1857.*

"I feel it needful for me to be particularly cautious whenever I come to any meeting in the city which has to deal with money and monetary affairs. It is seldom that I appear at all in these regions, unless, indeed, it be occasionally to pay a pleasing visit to Messrs. Bradbury and Evans, in Bouverie Street, or to Messrs. Smith and Co., of Cornhill. But I read my paper like every good Briton, and from that I gather a lesson of profound caution in speaking to mercantile men on subjects of this kind. Supposing, for instance, that I have shares in the Bundelcund Banking

* Mr. Thackeray was in the chair at the Commercial Travellers' Dinner, in 1857.

Company, or in the Royal British Diddlesex Bank: I come down to a meeting of the shareholders, and hear an honoured treasurer and an admirable president make the most flourishing reports of the state of our concern, showing to us enormous dividends accompanied with the most elegant bonuses; and proving to us that our funds are invested in the most secure way at Bogleywallak, Bundelcund, and Branksea Castle. I go away delighted at the happy prospect before my wife and family, feeling perfect confidence that those innocent beings will be comfortable for the rest of their lives. What, then, is my horror when, in one brief fortnight after, instead of those enormous dividends and elegant bonuses, I am served with a notice to pay up a most prodigious sum; when I find that our estates at Bundelcund and Bogleywallak have been ravaged by the Bengal tiger; that the island of Branksea is under water; that our respected president is obliged to go to Spain for the benefit of his health, and our eloquent treasurer cannot abide the London fog. You see I must be a little careful. But, granted that the accounts we have here have not, like our dinner, been subjected to an ingenious culinary process; granted that you have spent, as I read in your report, 25,000*l.* in raising a noble school and grounds; that you have collected around you the happy juvenile faces which I see smiling on yonder benches, to be the objects of your Christian kindness; granting all this to be true, then, gentlemen, I am your most humble servant, and no words that I can find can express my enthusiastic admiration for what you have done. I sincerely wish, on behalf of my own class, the literary profession, that we could boast of anything as good. I wish that we had an institution to which we could confide our children, instead of having to send them about to schools as we do, at an awful cost. When the respected Mr. Squeers of Dothe-boys Hall, announces that he proposes to take a limited number of pupils—I should rather say a number of very limited pupils—it is not because he is in love with the little darlings that he does it, but because he designs to extract a profit out of them. It always pains me to think of the profits to be screwed out of the bellies of the poor little innocents. Why have we not, as men of letters, some such association as that which you have got up? I appeal to my literary brethren, if any of them are present, whether we, the men of the line, cannot emulate the men of the road? A week ago, a friend engaged in my own profession, making his 1,000*l.* a year, showed me his half-yearly account of his two little boys at school. These little heroes of six and seven, who are at a very excellent school, where they are well provided for, came home with a little bill in their pocket which amounted to the sum of 75*l.* for the half year. Now think of this poor Paterfamilias earning his moderate 1,000*l.* a year, out of which he has his life assurance, his income-tax, and his house-rent to pay, with three or four poor relations to support—for doubtless we are all blessed with those appendages—with the heavy bills of his wife and daughters for millinery and mantua-making, to meet, especially at their present enormous rates and sizes. Think of this over-burdened man having to pay 75*l.* for one half-year's schooling of his little boys! Let the gentlemen of the press, then, try to devise some scheme which shall benefit them, as you have undoubtedly benefited by what you have accomplished for yourselves. We are all travellers and voyagers who must embark on life's ocean; and before you send your boys to sea you teach them to swim, to navigate the ship, and guide her into port. The last time I visited America, two years ago, I sailed on board the *Africa*, Captain Harrison. As she was steaming out of Liverpool one fine blowy October day, and was hardly over the bar, when, animated by those peculiar sensations not uncommon to landsmen at the commencement of a sea voyage, I was holding on amidships (a laugh), up comes a quick-eyed shrewd-looking little man, who holds on to the next rope to me, and says, "Mr. Thackeray, I am the representative of the house of Appleton and Co., of Broadway, New York—a most liberal and enterprising publishing firm, who will be most happy to do business with you." I don't know that we then did any business in the line thus delicately hinted at, because at that particular juncture we were both of us called, by a heavy lurch of the ship, to a casting-up of accounts of a far less agreeable character."

IN MEMORIAM.

By Charles Dickens.

It has been desired by some of the personal friends of the great English writer who established this magazine, that its brief record of his having been stricken from among men should be written by the old comrade and brother in arms who pens these lines, and of whom he often wrote himself, and always with the warmest generosity.

I saw him first, nearly twenty-eight years ago, when he proposed to become the illustrator of my earliest book. I saw him last, shortly before Christmas, at the Athenæum Club, when he told me that he had been in bed three days—that, after these attacks, he was troubled with cold shiverings, "which quite took the power of work out of him"—and that he had it in his mind to try a new remedy which he laughingly described.

He was very cheerful and looked very bright. In the night of that day week, he died.

The long interval between those two periods is marked in my remembrance of him by many occasions when he was supremely humorous, when he was irresistibly extravagant, when he was softened and serious, when he was charming with children. But, by none do I recall him more tenderly than by two or three that start out of the crowd, when he unexpectedly presented himself in my room, announcing how that some passage in a certain book had made him cry yesterday, and how that he had come to dinner, "because he couldn't help it," and must talk such passage over. No one can ever have seen him more genial, natural, cordial, fresh, and honestly impulsive, than I have seen him at these times. No one can be surer than I, of the greatness and the goodness of the heart that then disclosed itself.

We had our differences of opinion. I thought that he too much feigned a want of earnestness, and that he made a pretence of undervaluing his art, which was not good for the art that he held in trust. But, when we fell upon these topics, it was never very gravely, and I have a lively image of him in my mind, twisting both his hands in his hair, and stamping about, laughing, to make an end of the discussion.

When we were associated in remembrance of the late Mr. Douglas Jerrold, he delivered a public lecture in London, in the course of which, he read his very best contribution to PUNCH, describing the grown-up cares of a poor family of young children. No one hearing him could have doubted his natural gentleness, or his thoroughly unaffected manly sympathy with the weak and lowly. He read the paper most pathetically, and with a simplicity of tenderness that certainly moved one of his audience to tears. This was presently after his standing for Oxford, from which place he had dispatched his agent to me, with a droll note (to which he afterwards added a verbal postscript), urging me to "come down and make a speech, and tell them who he was, for he doubted whether more than two of the electors had ever heard of him, and he thought there might be as many as six or eight who had heard of me." He introduced the lecture just mentioned, with a reference to his late electioneering failure, which was full of good sense, good spirits, and good humour.

He had a particular delight in boys, and an excellent way with them. I remember his once asking me with fantastic gravity, when he had been to Eton where my eldest son then was, whether I felt as he did in regard of never seeing a boy without wanting instantly to give him a sovereign? I thought of this when I looked down into his grave, after he was laid there, for I looked down into it over the shoulder of a boy to whom he had been kind.

These are slight remembrances; but it is to little familiar things suggestive of the voice, look, manner, never, never more to be encountered on this earth, that the mind first turns in a bereavement. And greater things that are known of him, in the way of his warm affections, his quiet endurance, his unselfish thoughtfulness for others, and his munificent hand, may not be told.

If, in the reckless vivacity of his youth, his satirical pen had ever gone astray or done amiss, he had caused it to prefer its own petition for forgiveness, long before :

> I've writ the foolish fancy of his brain;
> The aimless jest that, striking, hath caused pain;
> The idle word that he'd wish back again.

In no pages should I take it upon myself at this time to discourse of his books, of his refined knowledge of character, of his subtle acquaintance with the weaknesses of human nature, of his delightful playfulness as an essayist, of his quaint and touching ballads, of his mastery over the English language. Least of all, in these pages, enriched by his brilliant qualities from the first of the series, and beforehand accepted by the Public through the strength of his great name.

But, on the table before me, there lies all that he had written of his latest and last story. That it would be very sad to any one—that it is inexpressibly so to a writer—in its evidences of matured designs never to be accomplished, of intentions begun to be executed and destined never to be completed, of careful preparation for long roads of thought that he was never to traverse, and for shining goals that he was never to reach, will be readily believed. The pain, however, that I have felt in perusing it, has not been deeper than the conviction that he was in the healthiest vigour of his powers when he wrought on this last labour. In respect of earnest feeling, far-seeing purpose, character, incident, and a certain loving picturesqueness blending the whole, I believe it to be much the best of all his works. That he fully meant it to be so, that he had become strongly attached to it, and that he bestowed great pains upon it, I trace in almost every page. It contains one picture which must have caused him extreme distress, and which is a masterpiece. There are two children in it, touched with a hand as loving and tender as ever a father caressed his little child with. There is some young love, as pure and innocent and pretty as the truth. And it is very remarkable that, by reason of the singular construction of the story, more than one main incident usually belonging to the end of such a fiction is anticipated in the beginning, and thus there is an approach to completeness in the fragment, as to the satisfaction of the reader's mind concerning the most interesting persons, which could hardly have been better attained if the writer's breaking-off had been foreseen.

The last line he wrote, and the last proof he corrected, are among these papers through which I have so sorrowfully made my way. The condition of the little pages of manuscript where Death stopped his hand, shows that he had carried them about, and often taken them out of his pocket here and there, for patient revision and interlineation. The last words he corrected in print, were, "And my heart throbbed with exquisite bliss." GOD grant that on that Christmas Eve when he laid his head back on his pillow and threw up his arms as he had been wont to do when very weary, some consciousness of duty done and Christian hope throughout life humbly cherished, may have caused his own heart so to throb, when he passed away to his Redeemer's rest!

He was found peacefully lying as above described, composed, undisturbed, and to all appearance asleep, on the twenty-fourth of December, 1863. He was only in his fifty-third year; so young a man, that the mother who blessed him in his first sleep, blessed him in his last. Twenty years before, he had written, after being in a white squall:

> And when, its force expended,
> The harmless storm was ended,
> And, as the sunrise splendid
>   Came blushing o'er the sea;
> I thought, as day was breaking,
> My little girls were waking,
> And smiling, and making
>   A prayer at home for me.

Those little girls had grown to be women when the mournful day broke that saw their father lying dead. In those twenty years of companionship with him, they had learned much from him; and one of them has a literary course before her, worthy of her famous name.

On the bright wintry day, the last but one of the old year, he was laid in his grave at Kensal Green, there to mingle the dust to which the mortal part of him had returned, with that of a third child, lost in her infancy, years ago. The heads of a great concourse of his fellow-workers in the Arts, were bowed around his tomb.

W. M. THACKERAY.

By Anthony Trollope.

"Quis desiderio sit pudor aut modus Tam cari capitis?—What shame to wail with tears the loss of so dear a head, or when will there be an end to such weeping?" Now, at the present moment, it is not so much that he who has left us was known, admired, and valued, as that he was loved. The fine grey head, the dear face with its gentle smile, the sweet, manly voice which we knew so well, with its few words of kindest greeting; the gait, the manner, and personal presence of him whom it so delighted us to encounter in our casual comings and goings about the town—it is of these things, of these things lost for ever, that we are now thinking! We think of them as of treasures which are not only lost, but which can never be replaced. He who knew Thackeray will have a vacancy in his heart's inmost casket, which must remain vacant till he dies. One loved him almost as one loves a woman, tenderly and with thoughtfulness—thinking of him when away from him as a source of joy which cannot be analysed, but is full of comfort. One who loved him, loved him thus because his heart was tender, as is the heart of a woman.

It need be told to no one that four years ago —four years and one month at the day on which these words will come before the reader—this Magazine was commenced under the guidance, and in the hands, of Mr. Thackeray. It is not for any of us who were connected with him in the enterprise to say whether this was done successfully or not; but it is for us—for us of all men— to declare that he was the kindest of guides, the gentlest of rulers, and, as a fellow-workman, liberal, unselfish, considerate, beyond compare. It has been said of him that he was jealous as a writer. We of the *Cornhill* knew nothing of such jealousy. At the end of two years Mr. Thackeray gave up the management of the Magazine, finding that there was much in the very nature of the task which embarrassed and annoyed him. He could not bear to tell an ambitious aspirant that his aspirations were in vain; and worse again, he could not endure to do so when a lady was his suppliant. Their letters to him were thorns that festered in his side, as he has told us himself. In truth it was so. There are many who delight in wielding the editorial ferule, good men and true, no doubt, who open their hearts genially to genius when they find it; but they can repress and crush the incapable tyro, or the would-be poetess who has nothing to support her but her own ambition, if not with delight, at least with satisfaction. Of such men are good editors made. Whether it be a point against a man, or for him, to be without such power, they who think of the subject may judge for themselves. Thackeray had it not. He lacked hardness for the place, and therefore, at the end of two years, he relinquished it.

But he did not on that account in any way sever himself from the Magazine. His *Roundabout Papers*, the first of which appeared in our first number, were carried on through 1862, and were completed in the early part of 1863. *Lovel the Widower*, and his *Lectures on the Four Georges*, appeared under his own editorship. *Philip* was so commenced, but was completed after he had ceased to reign. It was only in November last, as our readers may remember, that a paper appeared from his hand, entitled, *Strange to say, on Club Paper*. In this he ridiculed a silly report as to Lord Clyde, which had spread itself about the town,—doing so with that mingled tenderness and sarcasm for which he was noted,—the tenderness being ever for those named, and the sarcasm for those unknown. As far as we know, they were the last words he lived to publish. Speaking of the old hero who has just gone he bids us remember that "censure and praise are alike to him;—'The music warbling to the deafened ear, The incense wasted on the funeral bier!'" How strange and how sad that these, his last words, should now come home to us as so fitted for himself! Not that we believe that such praise is wasted,—even on the spirit of him who has gone.

> Comes the blind Fury with abhorred shears,
> And slits the thin spun life! "But not the praise,"
> Phœbus replied, and touched my trembling ears.

Why should the dead be inaccessible to the glory given to them by those who follow them on the earth? He, of whom we speak, loved such incense when living. If that be an infirmity he was so far infirm. But we hold it to be no infirmity. Who is the man who loves it not? Where is the public character to whom it is not as the breath of his nostrils? But there are men to whom it is given to conceal their feelings. Of such Thackeray was not one. He carried his heart-strings in a crystal case, and when they were wrung or when they were soothed all their workings were seen by friend and foe.

When he died he was still at work for this Magazine. He was writing yet another novel for the delight of its readers. "Shall we continue this story-telling business and be voluble to the end of our age? Will it not be presently time, O prattler, to hold your tongue and let younger people speak?" These words, of course, were his own. You will find them in that Roundabout

Paper of his, *De Finibus*, which was printed in August, 1862. He was voluble to the end;—alas, that it should have been the end! The leisure time of which he was thinking never came to him. That presently was denied to him, nor had he lived would it have been his for many a year to come. He was young in power, young in heart as a child, young even in constitution in spite of that malady which carried him off. But, though it was so, Thackeray ever spoke of himself, and thought of himself, as of one that was old. He in truth believed that the time for letting others speak was speedily coming to him. But they who knew him did not believe it, and his forthcoming new novel was anxiously looked for by many who expected another *Esmond*.

I may not say how great the loss will be to the *Cornhill*, but I think that those concerned in the matter will be adjudged to be right in giving to the public so much of this work as he has left behind him. A portion of a novel has not usually much attraction for general readers; but we venture to think that this portion will attract. They who have studied Mr. Thackeray's characters in fiction,—and it cannot be doubted that they have become matter of study to many,—will wish to follow him to the last, and will trace with a sad but living interest the first rough lines of the closing portraits from his hand.

I shall not attempt here any memoir of Mr. Thackeray's life. Such notices as the passing day requires have been given in many of the daily and weekly papers, and have been given, I believe, correctly. I may, perhaps, specially notice that from the pen of Mr. Hannay, which appeared in the *Edinburgh Courant.* The writing of his life will be a task, and we trust a work of love, for which there will probably be more than one candidate. We trust that it may fall into fitting hands,—into the hands of one who shall have loved wisely, and not too well,—but, above all things, into the hands of a true critic. That which the world will most want to know of Thackeray, is the effect which his writings have produced; we believe that effect to have been very wide, and beneficial withal. Let us hope, also, that the task of his biography may escape the untoward hurry which has ruined the interest of so many of the memoirs of our latter-day worthies.

Of our late Editor's works, the best known, and most widely appreciated are, no doubt, *Vanity Fair*, *Pendennis*, *The Newcomes*, and *Esmond*. The first on the list has been the most widely popular with the world at large. *Pendennis* has been the best loved by those who have felt and tasted the delicacy of Thackeray's tenderness. *The Newcomes* stands conspicuously for the character of the Colonel, who as an English gentleman has no equal in English fiction. *Esmond*, of all his works, has most completely satisfied the critical tastes of those who profess themselves to read critically. For myself, I own that I regard *Esmond* as the first and finest novel in the English language. Taken as a whole, I think that it is without a peer. There is in it a completeness of historical plot, and an absence of that taint of unnatural life which blemishes, perhaps, all our other historical novels, which places it above its brethren. And, beyond this, it is replete with a tenderness which is almost divine,—a tenderness which no poetry has surpassed. Let those who doubt this go back and study again the life of Lady Castlewood. In *Esmond*, above all his works, Thackeray achieves the great triumph of touching the innermost core of his subject, without ever wounding the taste. We catch all the aroma, but the palpable body of the thing never stays with us till it palls us. Who ever wrote of love with more delicacy than Thackeray has written in *Esmond*. May I quote one passage of three or four lines? Who is there that does not remember the meeting between Lady Castlewood and Harry Esmond after Esmond's return. "'Do you know what day it is?' she continued. 'It is the 29th December; it is your birthday! But last year we did not drink it;—no, no! My lord was cold, and my Harry was like to die; and my brain was in a fever; and we had no wine. But now,—now you are come again, bringing your sheaves with you, my dear.' She burst into a wild flood of weeping as she spoke; she laughed and sobbed on the young man's heart, crying out wildly;—'bringing your sheaves with you,—your sheaves with you!'"

But if *Esmond* be, as a whole, our best English novel, Colonel Newcome is the finest single character in English fiction. That it has been surpassed by Cervantes, in *Don Quixote*, we may, perhaps, allow, though *Don Quixote* has the advantage of that hundred years which is necessary to the perfect mellowing of any great work. When Colonel Newcome shall have lived his hundred years, and the lesser works of Thackeray and his compeers shall have died away, then, and not till then, will the proper rank of this creation in literature be appreciated.

We saw him laid low in his simple grave at the close of last year, and we saw the brethren of his art, one after another, stand up on the stone at the grave foot to take a last look upon the coffin which held him. It was very sad. There were the faces of rough men red with tears, who are not used to the melting mood. The grave was very simple, as became the sadness of the moment. At such times it is better that the very act of interment should be without pomp or sign of glory. But as weeks pass by us, they, who love English literature, will desire to see some preparation for placing a memento of him in that shrine in which we keep the monuments of our great men. It is to be regarded as a thing of course, that there should be a bust of Thackeray in Westminster Abbey.

THE END.

www.ingramcontent.com/pod-product-compliance
Lightning Source LLC
Chambersburg PA
CBHW020758230426
43666CB00007B/752